STORMIE OMARTIAN

PRAYER WARRIOR

HARVEST HOUSE PUBLISHERS
EUGENE, OREGON

PRAYER WARRIOR
Copyright © 2013 by Stormie Omartian
Published by Harvest House Publishers
Eugene, Oregon 97402
www.harvesthousepublishers.com

Library of Congress Cataloging-in-Publication Data
Omartian, Stormie.
Prayer warrior / Stormie Omartian.
    pages cm
ISBN 978-0-7369-5366-5 (pbk.)
ISBN 978-0-7369-5556-0 (Deluxe)
ISBN 978-0-7369-5367-2 (eBook)
1. Prayer—Christianity. I. Title.
BV215.O54 2013
248.3'2—dc23
                                                      2013014357

This book is dedicated to the prayer warriors all over the world—especially those who have come up to me wherever I have been and whispered, "I am a prayer warrior too."

*You know who you are, but you will never know
how much that warmed my heart,
and how thankful I am that you
are with me on the wall.*

CONTENTS

You are of God, little children,
and have overcome them,
because He who is in you is greater
than he who is in the world.

1 JOHN 4:4

1

UNDERSTAND THERE IS A WAR AND YOU ARE IN IT

I lived in Southern California for more than four decades, and I was present for the worst earthquakes of that period. I never got used to them. They were more terrifying to me than anything else. That's because they happened suddenly, without any warning whatsoever, and you had no idea how long they would last, how strong they would be, or how much damage they would do. Some earthquakes were so violent I couldn't even get to a doorway or under a solid table as we were instructed to do. At times like those, when a strong earthquake is happening, your life feels totally out of control. You don't know if you are going to be killed, buried alive, or badly injured. Or, you hope, escape with none of the above occurring.

The buildings that survived those big earthquakes had a secure foundation and were especially fortified to withstand violent shaking. When California eventually established specific building codes that made buildings safer in an earthquake, wise people became aware of which buildings those were and whether or not they were in one.

The most dreaded situation was when an earthquake happened in the dark of night while you were sleeping. It was a rude awakening to pitch black because the power went out and you could see absolutely nothing. Even if the power did *not* go out, there was no way you could get to a source of light while the room was shaking violently unless you kept a flashlight under your pillow. Even then, trying to grab hold of it could be nearly impossible, depending on the magnitude.

The worst earthquake I remember enduring happened when I was living alone in an apartment in Studio City, just over Laurel Canyon from Hollywood. It happened in the middle of the night while I was sound asleep in my bedroom. I lived on the bottom floor of a two-story, four-apartment complex, built before earthquake building codes were established and implemented. Even though there was only one story above me, I knew that it was possible my apartment could collapse under the weight of that floor. If the top apartment fell in on mine, it would be over for me. Years before, I had seen the wreckage of that exact thing with my own eyes *after* it happened, and I never forgot it.

All of that was crystal clear in my mind when this earthquake hit, which was sudden, violent, and loud. I tried to make my way out of the bedroom and down the short hallway to the door leading into the living room, because at least from there I might have a shot at getting out the front door to the lawn and away from anything falling in the aftershocks. But too many windows were in the living room at the front of the apartment, including the French windows in the top half of the front door, to try and attempt an escape while the ground was still violently shaking. I thought if I could be as close as possible to that front door without getting hit by flying glass, perhaps I could manage to get out before the whole building went down. Judging by the extreme shaking of the apartment, a collapse seemed an imminent possibility.

As I stumbled down the short hallway, I was thrown violently against the walls from side to side, hitting my right and then my left shoulder hard each time. Over the deafening rumble of the earthquake and shaking of the building, I could hear my dishes falling out of the cabinets in the kitchen and crashing to the floor. My lamps hit hard against the walls. Every second seems like eternity when the earth and everything around you is shaking, especially if you are not in a place that is built on a solid foundation and according to proven and reliable building codes.

I did not have a personal relationship with God at the time this happened, but I desperately tried to establish one in that moment. Yet God felt distant and preoccupied. Being terrified and alone had become a way of life for me, having been raised by an out-of-control, mentally ill mother on an isolated ranch in Wyoming miles from the nearest neighbor or town. But enduring her abuse and being locked in a closet whenever my dad was gone didn't compare with this earthquake experience. At least in the closet I had the hope of getting out. I didn't think I would get out of this quake alive, and I had no one to *pray* to or *turn* to.

I certainly did not have that place of peace that can be found in the Lord even in terrifying circumstances. In fact, at that time I'd never heard of such a thing.

I did get out of that earthquake without serious injury, but the moment the shaking stopped I grabbed my purse and car keys and left to go stay with a friend before the aftershocks began. It was way too dangerous and frightening to stay another moment there because the place could still collapse.

On the way to my friend's house, the aftershocks were so violent that my car was thrown all over the road as though it were a toy. Talk about a wild ride. You haven't lived until you have driven a car while the pavement below it is rolling up and down like a thin sheet in a violent windstorm and cracking in such deep fissures that you fear being swallowed into one. I was frightened out of my mind. Aftershocks can be just as scary as the earthquake itself, especially because you know everything around you is already weakened.

I stayed with my friend for days until the aftershocks stopped. Then, as soon as I felt safe enough to pick up the pieces in my apartment, I packed up what wasn't broken and moved out. It wasn't long after that I ended up marrying someone just so I wouldn't ever have to be that alone and terrified again. The marriage didn't even survive two years. In the second year I received the Lord, and my husband did not like that and declared in no uncertain terms that I was not allowed to ever say the name of Jesus in his house. That was like saying to someone dying of thirst that they were never allowed to have water again. It was the final straw in a disastrous marriage. We could not reconcile after that. I was alone again, but for the first time in my life I felt as though I wasn't. I had been dead, but now I was alive. And I had found a well of living water that never runs dry.

Over the years since then, I have realized that our spiritual life is much like my circumstances were at the time of that earthquake. If we have not built it on a solid foundation, according to proven and strong building codes, then we are unable to stand secure and unharmed in the shaking and upheavals that are going on *in* us and *around* us. And who among us have not felt such shaking? Everything seems unstable in our world—the weather, governments, environment, work, relationships, health, marriage, children, mind, and emotions—the list is endless. But the truth is that even though these things are happening *around* us or *to* us, we can have more control over our life than most people believe. But it takes having the right foundation and building according to a specific code.

How to Build a Solid Foundation

First of all, we were never intended to build our life alone. We are not meant to take everything into our own hands in order to make our life be what we want it to be. Our life was not made to be out of control. Nor were we formed to live in fear. Instead, each one of us is created to be under *God's* control. We are meant to *surrender* our life to the Lord and invite Him to make us everything *He created* us to be. We were made to walk with Him in every situation, enjoying

His peace that passes all understanding. It is possible to establish our life on such a solid foundation that no matter what is happening around us, *we will not be shaken.*

In order to do that, our life must be built on the Rock. The Bible says, "No other foundation can anyone lay than that which is laid, which is Jesus Christ" (1 Corinthians 3:11).

Jesus said, "Whoever comes to Me, and hears My sayings and does them, I will show you whom he is like: He is like a man building a house, who dug deep and *laid the foundation on the rock.* And when the flood arose, the stream beat vehemently against that house, and *could not shake it, for it was founded on the rock*" (Luke 6:47-48).

The solid Rock is Jesus. His presence in your life affects every aspect of it.

The solid Rock is also the Word of God. Jesus is called the *living Word.* That's because Jesus *is* the Word. Jesus and His Word are inseparable. You can't have one without the other. Jesus and His Word are the solid foundation upon which we can build and establish our life.

When we receive Jesus, He gives us His Holy Spirit to live in us, which is the seal indicating we belong to Him. The Holy Spirit enables us to live out what the Word teaches. It is the way God changes us and works deeply in our hearts to establish, secure, and strengthen us. Jesus—the Word of God—and God's Holy Spirit in us help us to stand strong, no matter how much everything around us is shaking, collapsing, and falling. (More about all that in chapter 2, "Know Your Commander and Stand on His Side.")

There Is a War Going On

If you are a believer in Jesus and have received Him as your Savior, you are in the body of Christ. This means you are in the spiritual war between God and His enemy. Even if you have *not* yet received Jesus, you are still in the war. You just don't know it yet and therefore have no control over the things that happen to you. You can be hit and hurt in the cross fire from the enemy of your soul and not realize what's happening. You could be suffering with problems—one accident or disease after another; the failure of a marriage, trouble with relationships, problems at work, or financial trouble; mental torment; the consequences of bad decisions; the rebellion of children— again, the list is endless. You may think it's just bad luck, but it's not. It's cross fire from an enemy you don't know you have.

Believers can suffer from cross fire too, but that's because they don't understand a war is going on and they are in it. Far too many believers are being knocked around by the enemy of their soul and their life, but they think bad things just happen to them because that's the way life is. So they are not actively engaged in the war, even though they are on the receiving end of the consequences of that war. They are attacked and become wounded and incapacitated because they are totally unprepared to face enemy opposition. They are completely uninformed about how to do battle.

God's Enemy Is Your Enemy

You may think you are not at war with anyone, but you don't have to be at war with someone in order for them to be at war with *you*. You can *think* your spiritual enemy doesn't exist and therefore you are not at war with him, but the truth is that no matter what you think, you have an enemy who is always opposing you. One of his favorite ploys is to convince you he doesn't exist, and therefore he is not a threat. He is a master of disguise. He even disguises himself as an angel of light. Imagine how misleading that can be if you are unable to identify a counterfeit.

You may be thinking, *I don't want to think about or talk about the enemy.* I don't either. And we don't have to…much. But we had certainly better acknowledge that he exists, and that he is hell-bent on destroying us. We had better realize that just as God has a plan for our lives, the enemy has a plan for our lives too. And that is to rob, kill, and destroy us. We must also recognize that God has given us a way to take dominion over the enemy and his evil works of darkness in our lives. Because if we don't understand this, if we ignore the enemy or pretend he doesn't exist, then *his* plans can succeed.

As a believer, you are already involved in spiritual warfare whether you realize it, know it, accept it, or recognize it. You may think that some of the difficult things that happen to you or to others, or that are evident in the situations in the world around you, are mere coincidence or bad luck, but it is far more sinister than that. Those things are the result of planning by an enemy, and he is the enemy of God and of all God's children. This means you and me. You may think you are not in the war, but you are. You may believe you don't have to engage in the battle, but you do. Too often when people contend in prayer for the will of the Lord to prevail in a specific battle, they think that once the battle is won the war is over. *But the war is never over because the enemy never has a good day and is feeling kindly toward you.*

You can push that reality away from you, but it is still there. And then one day you find that bad things are happening to *you.* You are being shaken and it is severely affecting *your* life, and you are not prepared to do anything about it.

How you respond to the enemy of your soul determines whether his plan for your life or God's plan for your life is realized.

Most believers recognize they have an enemy. They have read the Bible and they know that part. And they pray for God's will to prevail. But there are many battles in life, and God calls those of us who are believers in Him to go to battle as prayer warriors for His kingdom. This is not just a select few. Not just the most spiritual. Not just the ones who like that kind of thing or have nothing else to do. He calls *all* believers to be active in spiritual warfare. You might say you've been born again into God's army.

We cannot afford the luxury of foolishly thinking, *If I don't acknowledge I have an enemy, then I won't ever have to engage with him in any way. I can stay out of the war completely.* If that is you, may I politely say this to you in love: *You are dreaming! You are living in a fantasy!* The enemy has a plan for your life and so does God. Which plan do you want to succeed? God gives you a free will and allows you to choose *His* will in your life. The enemy doesn't care a whit about your free will as long as he can influence you to bend it in the direction of his plan for your destruction. I know people who believe if they never acknowledge that the enemy even exists—and especially if they don't allow for the fact that *God's* enemy is *their* enemy as well—then they will never be drawn into any battle, let alone a war. But those who deny the war, refuse to see it, ignore it, or run from it are destined to lose it.

Allow me to repeat myself.

The truth is that we are already in the war. The war is never over until we go to be with the Lord. Better to stand and fight the way God wants us to.

I've read the entire Bible many times, and I know the end of the story. In the war between God and His enemy, God wins. This is not like earthly wars where people hope and pray they win. In this war we have victory over the enemy, but we still have to fight each battle in order to see victory happen.

Every battle is waged in prayer.

Prayer is the actual battle.

During World War II pictures were displayed everywhere that showed a man dressed in red, white, and blue trousers and tails pointing directly at you as you looked at the photo. The caption said, "Uncle Sam Wants You." Uncle Sam—meaning the United States—wanted men and women to fight in the military. There is a similar image you need to picture in your mind, and that is a picture of Jesus looking at you and pointing His finger toward you, saying, "Father God Wants You." God wants you to fight in His army. Will you answer that call?

You don't have to be afraid of battle terminology. There is no reason to fear words such as "warrior," "war," "weapons," and "warfare." This is a spiritual battle. It is every bit as real as the fleshly battles waged on earth today, but in a spiritual war the way you do battle is to pray. That's not scary. God's army is the only one where you can be deployed but you don't actually have to go anywhere. The moment you say, "Count me in, Lord. I want to join with other prayer warriors to see Your will done on earth," you are on active duty. When God puts a person, group of people, neighborhood, city, or a foreign land on your heart, He has connected you to them in the Spirit and you can intercede on their behalf. You are active as a prayer warrior the moment you put words to your heartfelt feelings and talk to God about them. Your heart will be deployed to wherever God sends you in prayer.

The Heart of a Prayer Warrior

If you are a person who thinks you may not have what it takes to be a prayer warrior, or if you are concerned that being a prayer warrior is too difficult, or if you believe you don't have time for it, let me ask you the following questions:

Do you see people suffering and it bothers you? Do you want to do something to alleviate that suffering and feel unable to do enough? If so, then you have the heart of a prayer warrior.

Do you recognize evil proliferating in the world? Do you long to find some way to stop this destruction in people's lives? If so, then you have the heart of a prayer warrior.

Do you experience any injustice in your life or can you identify it in the lives of others? Do you see injustice marching forth in a seemingly unstoppable advance? Does it upset you and you would like to have a way to change that? If so, then you have the heart of a prayer warrior.

Do you observe wrong things happening around you and you want to right them? Do you recognize the culture of hate growing stronger and you are troubled by it? If so, then you have the heart of a prayer warrior.

Do you ever have a certain person heavy on your heart and it concerns you, but you are not sure why? Do you know people who are going through terribly difficult situations and you want to do something to help them but don't know how? If so, then you have the heart of a prayer warrior.

Do you observe tragic situations happening to people and feel helpless to do anything to stop them? Do you ever wish you could have done something that might have prevented such tragedy? If so, then you have the heart of a prayer warrior.

Do you become grieved in your spirit when you see blatant disregard for God and His ways? Do you have sympathy for people who don't recognize their need for the Lord, yet you feel powerless to affect their lives in any way? If so, you have the heart of a prayer warrior.

In fact, if you said yes to *any* of the questions above, then you have the heart of a prayer warrior. Becoming a prayer warrior *begins* in the heart, sometimes without your even being aware of it.

A prayer warrior has a heart of compassion for suffering people and bad situations, and desires to do something to make a difference.

When you tell God you are reporting for service as His prayer warrior, He will put specific people or situations on your heart that He wants you to pray about. You don't have to go searching for them—unless you feel led to do so—because those needs will be quickly made known to you. For example, like you, I have many situations and people on my heart that concern me. Aside from going to battle in prayer for my own life and the lives of my family members, friends, neighbors, coworkers, and specific individuals I know of who need someone to stand up for them in prayer regarding the things they are facing, there are serious problems for others in the world that stand out in my heart above all the rest.

One example is that I cannot tolerate children being hurt. I can't bear to hear of one more child who has been kidnapped, abused, molested, or murdered. So whenever God brings that kind of situation to my mind, I pray for children to be protected. I pray that anyone who hurts a child in any way will be put in jail and not released to do harm again. I pray for child abusers and molesters to be revealed and caught *before* they succeed with their hellish plans. I pray specifically that people who are involved in the rescue of such children will be able to capture evil perpetrators *before* they can strike again. I have acknowledged before God that I am in His service as a prayer warrior, and I know He has put this on my heart in a big way.

Another issue strongly on my heart is the sex slavery market. I find it unthinkable that men with hearts overtaken by evil and greed will capture young boys and girls and sell them to other men who would actually pay to abuse them in order to satisfy their own sick, selfish, and despicable desires. No decent human being can know this is going on and say there is no evil in the world. So I pray that God will open up a means of escape for these young victims by sending godly people who will help them leave this life of hell and find the restoration the Lord has for them. I pray for the workers who are trying to set these young people free to have the favor of God and miraculous success. I pray that the evil men involved in this travesty be exposed, convicted in every possible way, and their works from hell destroyed.

How can we know things like these are happening and *not* pray?

As prayer warriors, we must remember that no matter how hopeless a situation may appear to us, God gives us power in prayer to do something about it. *We* may be overwhelmed by it, but *God* is *not*. We may not see a way out, but *God* can. Because of Him, we *can* make a *difference*!

You May Pray Alone but You Don't Fight Alone

The only reason the world enjoys whatever peace and blessing it does is because godly men and women are praying. Most people have no idea about that. They go along merrily, not in the least bit aware they are enjoying the fruit, blessing, safety, happiness, and success they have because of people who take prayer seriously. They think it is because of good karma, good luck, or good genes (yes, I have actually heard people tell me that). But their good life is happening for none of those reasons. It is the result of the prayer warriors doing the work God has called them to do—to pray and intercede as His Holy Spirit leads them. And it is not just a few who are called. We are *all* called to pray. It is just that too few are listening. *You are* listening or you would not even be reading this.

After that horrendous earthquake I told you about, and after I became a believer, I found out that in Los Angeles there are many prayer warriors who pray specifically over the fault lines. They feel strongly led by the Holy Spirit to do so. They pray the "big one" that has been predicted for decades will not happen. Or if seismic shifting must happen, that there will be more small quakes instead. I talked to two women who were in such a group, and they actually go to the places where the fault lines are reported to be and pray there. I don't know how many people are praying like that in L.A. I didn't ask them. I was just talking about earthquakes one day, and these kind ladies told me about this. They were not seeking acclaim. They were just letting me know because I was concerned about earthquakes.

For years I wondered why more people weren't killed during earthquakes there, especially considering the violence of some of them. I believe now that it is God's response to the prayers of the prayer warriors. I have been in many bad earthquakes and yet have never been hurt. I do not think it was good luck, good karma, good genes, or even good sense that spared me. I give thanks to God for answering the prayers of the prayer warriors before I was ever aware that He or they existed.

I am not saying you have to do something as time-consuming or strenuous as the prayer warriors who go to the area of the fault lines. They knew they were called to do that. And believe me, when you are called to specific prayer, you won't be able to *not* do it. You won't roll your eyes at God and say, "Aw, do I have to? I'm tired. My favorite TV show is coming on now. I don't feel like it." Instead, you'll say, "Yes, Sir!" "Right away, Sir!" And you will count it a privilege to serve your great Commander that way. Even though you may be alone when you pray, you are not in the battle alone. Countless prayer warriors all over the world are praying with you.

The Time Is Later than We Think

We must get beyond praying just for our own needs. That doesn't mean we stop praying for them. Not at all. Jesus commanded us to pray about those things. And that is also part of being a prayer warrior. We must do battle in prayer for our own lives as well as the lives of our family members, friends, and the people God puts on our hearts. But we cannot stop there as if the rest of the world is not our problem. It is not only our problem to pray about, but we are *mandated* by the Lord to become the intercessors He is calling each one of us to be.

We can see evil encroaching all around us. We may be in a nice safe place right now, but that could change in an instant. Dreadful things are happening way too close to home.

My family and I used to live in what we thought was a safe neighborhood until one day it did not feel safe anymore. I could clearly *sense* evil moving in, even though I had no hard evidence at that time. I had been around enough evil in my life, especially in my younger years, to recognize it in my spirit the minute it came close. I prayed about it every day, but I could never shake the feeling that my husband and I and our children were not in a safe place. I prayed for God to deliver us from evil and push it back from our community.

The Holy Spirit led us to move away from there to someplace that felt safer. And not long after that it was uncovered in the community from where we had moved that an enormous child pornography ring was operating in a respectable-looking place right under everyone's noses. They brought in children and filmed horrendous displays of evil in our town and no one suspected it. We had all been aware of where pockets of evil and crime operated in that city and no one went near those areas, but we had no idea of what was being perpetrated in secret close to our own neighborhood.

After we left, a wonderful Christian lady we knew quite well was picking up her teenage daughter at a Bible study held in a house a couple blocks away from the house we had recently moved out of. While she waited with her young son outside in her car for her daughter to come out, a man pulled up behind her, got out of his car, walked up to her driver's side window, and pulled a gun on her. He demanded her purse and briefcase and she complied without resistance, but he shot her anyway. In cold blood. She died in front of her son and her daughter, who came running out of the house with the others at the Bible study. It was a terrible, horrific, unthinkable, heartbreaking tragedy no one should ever have experienced.

It took time, but eventually the man who shot that woman was caught, tried, and sentenced to life in prison. Justice was done, but no one felt safe in that neighborhood anymore. The truth is that no one is safe in any neighborhood anymore. Evil is everywhere, and we have to raise up a spiritual wall against it in prayer to keep it from moving into our neighborhood or community. Or if it is already there, we must pray to see it exposed and pushed back. That's what prayer warriors do.

I Don't Want to Be in a War—I Hate Violence

I know you don't want to be in a war. Neither do I. No one does. Countless people have said that throughout all of history. But you have no choice when the enemy attacks you. The fact that you hate violence is exactly the reason you must engage in the war. If you don't engage in the war first by praying *offensively*, the enemy will bring the battle to you. He will bring it to your home. Your neighborhood. Your school. Your place of work. Your movie theater. Your mall. The enemy comes to destroy, and when he does you must be ready to fight *defensively* in order to stop him. But the best way is to pray in advance to prevent it.

You may have picked up this book because you are curious about spiritual warfare—what it is and why anyone would want to be involved—but let me tell you that God wants to do more than satisfy your curiosity. What is going on all around you must be battled against and won in the spirit realm before it can be won on the ground.

This book will help you determine whose side you're on, who your Commander is, and how to recognize your true enemy. It will help you understand the authority you have in prayer, and how to condition yourself to be all God is calling you to be so you can stand strong. It will teach you how to put on your spiritual armor, become skilled with your weapons, identify the immediate battlefield, and engage in the war. It will show you how to resist the enemy, see each situation from God's perspective, and pray as the Holy Spirit leads you. When you do all of that, you will keep the enemy from taking anything that belongs to you, including your spouse, children, home, health, sanity, clarity, purity, peace, power, and close relationship with the Lord. You can also take back territory that belongs to God, such as people who are lost or cannot help themselves and need someone to stand strong against the enemy on their behalf.

God gives us dominion on the earth by the power of His Holy Spirit in us. But victory comes by doing battle every day with the enemy of all that is good. We are not supposed to sit by and allow problems to just happen to us. Yes, we will have struggles. They are often unavoidable. *God did not promise a life without trial or struggle.* He did not promise we would have instant victory over every challenge, but He has told us that when we proclaim His truth, and live His way and pray, we can overcome these problems. Our spiritual warfare in prayer prepares the way for God to bring victory.

This Sounds like Too Much Work

If you think being a prayer warrior sounds like too much work, let me tell you what is *really* too much work. Burying your child. Being called to the scene of a horrible accident. Getting a doctor's report about a terrible disease that you, a family member, or someone you know of has been diagnosed with. The dissolving of a close friendship. The severing of family ties. Bad relationships at work. Suffering from loneliness, sadness, frustration, hopelessness, or misery. Falling into debt, foreclosure, poverty, discouragement, sin, fear, dread, deep anxiety, or the breakup of a marriage. *All of that is too much work!*

You may be thinking, *Are you telling me all this happens when I don't pray?*

I'm asking you, can you tell me for certain that the enemy of your soul has nothing to do with any of this? That none of these problems are in any way part of his evil scheme for your demise? That he has nothing like this planned for your life or the lives of the people about whom you deeply care? Can you tell me that prayer has absolutely no affect upon any of these things I just mentioned?

Yes, we all do stupid things from time to time that get us into bad situations. And to some of us it can appear that these things *just happen*. But how many times do you wish you had prayed for someone you know *before* their tragic illness? Or their suicide? Or their drug overdose? Or their teenager's accident? Or their break-in? Too many, I'm sure. We all feel that. I'm *not* saying we are *responsible* when bad things happen because we didn't pray. I am saying bad things can be *prevented* when we do. And we *are* accountable to God for how *much* we pray, how *often* we pray, and how *fervently* we seek the leading of His Spirit as to *what* to pray.

The world around us is in a desperate situation. Suffering is increasing. We can *see* it. We know it. We *feel* it. And *that* is too much work! I become weary when I hear people say, "Well, if it's going to happen anyway, why pray?" Please hear me out on this. Yes, some things are certain. To list a few: the return of the Lord Jesus, the annihilation of the enemy's influence on earth, the rising up of the antichrist, and every prophecy in the Bible that has not already been fulfilled. But Jesus did not say to His believers, "Roll over and play dead until I come." He did not say, "These things are going to happen, so just eat, drink, and be merry until they do." No, He said we are to occupy where we are according to His will until He returns. We are to *worship Him, read His Word,* and *pray without ceasing* as long as we're here. When we *don't* do these things we are *out* of His will. There is no other way to see it. Far too much suffering happens because way too many people are not praying.

We have to wake up as the people of God. Prayer is how God works on earth. That is *His* idea, not mine. I am not just making this up; it is what the Bible says over and over. Countless good things will *not* happen unless people are praying about them. And terrible things *will* happen if we don't pray. God is asking us to listen for His leading.

The Bible says, "Bear one another's burdens, and so fulfill the law of Christ" (Galatians 6:2).

This, in a nutshell, is what it means to be a prayer warrior.

Take the burdens of other people to the Lord in prayer. That is intercession. Recognize the opposing work of the enemy and resist him in prayer. That is what prayer warriors do. Many storms have come, but many *more* storms *will* come. Things are shaking now, but much more *will* be shaken. If you have built on the Rock and are praying, you will stand firm and survive the storm. That is one of the many rewards of being a prayer warrior.

There is way too much to write about concerning spiritual warfare to fit it into one book. What I am writing about in this book is how you can become an effective prayer warrior. Or if you already *are* one, how you can become the most victorious prayer warrior possible. If we join together in prayer, we can break down every barrier to the unity God has called us all to and become the powerful army of prayer warriors He wants us to be.

Start by saying, "Lord, use me as Your prayer warrior," and the Holy Spirit will lead you from there.

Prayer for the Prayer Warrior

Lord, I pray You will help me build my life on a solid foundation. I know there is no more solid foundation than that which is built on the Rock—which is You, Jesus, and Your Word (1 Corinthians 3:11). No matter what is shaking around me, You give me a foundation that can never be shaken or destroyed.

Help me to always keep in mind that I am instrumental in the war between You and Your enemy, and victory in my life depends on my willingness to hear Your call to pray. I know this is spiritual warfare You want me to engage in, and prayer *is* the battle. Teach me to hear Your call and to pray in power the way You want me to.

Thank You, Lord, for the countless men and women whom You have called to be prayer warriors in this spiritual battle between good and evil, and who have already answered the call. I pray for the many who are still sitting on the sidelines, not realizing how they can become wounded by enemy fire. Help us all to wake up to Your truth. Enable us to bear one another's burdens in prayer and fulfill Your law (Galatians 6:2). Teach us all to always hear Your call.

Enable me to always hear the voice of Your Holy Spirit leading me to pray. Show me where my prayer is most needed for myself, my family, and the people and situations You put on my heart. Show me *how* I should pray. Help me to not think of prayer as merely asking You to fix things, but rather taking dominion over the works of darkness as You have said to do. Teach me to use the authority You have given me in prayer to advance Your kingdom on earth. Enable me to be part of stopping the spread of evil. Help me to advance Your kingdom in a powerful way.

In Jesus' name I pray.

Let us not sleep, as others do,
but let us watch and be sober.

1 THESSALONIANS 5:6

2

Know Your Commander and Stand on His Side

Every army has a commander who is the top leader. He is the one most trusted and skilled in knowing how to fight the war. Every soldier looks *to* him and all orders come *from* him. No good soldier would consider ignoring or disobeying his orders.

In human armies the soldiers may never know or even meet their commander. In God's spiritual army, you will not only meet your Commander, but you will meet Him *before* you become a warrior. That's because He wants you to not only know *about* Him, but He wants you to know Him well and have a deep relationship with Him that is close and personal. That means you don't just meet Him and it ends there. He wants you to *continue to grow* in your relationship with Him so that you can hear Him speaking to your heart. He wants you to always be able to clearly distinguish between *His* voice and that of the enemy. The better you know your Commander, and the more you look to Him for your strength, power, and guidance, the better a warrior you will be.

In a regular army your orders will come down through a chain of command. In the Lord's army there is no chain of command. You take your orders directly from your Commander.

Imagine you've decided to join the army and your Leader has already voluntarily agreed to die in your place so that you won't ever have to. Not only that, He has taken the consequences for any mistakes you have made in your life—or may make in the future—and given you a complete pardon so there will never be any need for a dishonorable discharge. Even if you were to do something terribly wrong, you could go to Him and confess the mistake and be forgiven and released from any charge that could be brought against you. How great is that?

Well, imagine no more. This is the way it is in the army of God because your Commander is Jesus. And He wants to have first place in your life.

Here are some things you must know about your Commander. Jesus was with God from the beginning (John 1:1-2). He came to earth—born as a man but still fully God—to free us from the forces of hell and the power of death. He was crucified on a cross, suffering death in our place. He rose again to prove He was who He said He was—the Son of God. He made the way for us to not only be saved for all eternity with Him, but also to be saved in this life from the hands of our enemy. He gave His life so that "*through death He might destroy him who had the power of death*, that is, the devil, and release those who through fear of death were all their lifetime subject to bondage" (Hebrews 2:14-15).

This means Jesus has freed us from the enemy who held the power of death over us. When Jesus died on the cross and was resurrected, He won absolute victory over death and hell. He suffered and died so we don't have to. He has delivered us from any reason to *fear* death, because when we die we will go to be with Him. We don't have to be afraid to die; we have to be afraid to live without Him.

We know as believers that "to be absent from the body" is "to be present with the Lord" (2 Corinthians 5:8). We also know that to be absent from the Lord as an unbeliever is no life at all.

The Bible says that Jesus was perfected through suffering (Hebrews 5:8-9). But that does not mean He was ever imperfect or sinful, for He was morally perfect. It means He *perfectly accomplished* what being a Savior for all people required of Him. In His suffering and death He became the perfect Savior. He perfectly fulfilled all He had to do to be the sacrifice for all of our sins. No one has ever done that but Him. No one else has ever died for you and rose from the dead to break the power of death and hell over you. Only Jesus. And that also makes Him the perfect Commander.

Jesus is actually the Commander of two armies. One is an army of angels in heaven and one is the army of prayer warriors on earth. In fact, Jesus is called "Lord Sabaoth." (No, that is not "Lord of the Sabbath" spelled wrong.) Lord Sabaoth means Commander of the armies of heaven and earth at war with Satan and his evil forces. As Commander of these two armies, Jesus shows us how to win control from the enemy over what he has stolen that is rightfully ours. Jesus secured our freedom from control of the enemy, but we still have to establish that liberty in our lives and in the lives of others. We do that in prayer as prayer warriors.

The following pages contain some other important things you need to know about your Commander.

Your Commander Chose You

The Bible says that God "*chose us* in Him before the foundation of the world, *that we should be holy and without blame* before Him in love, having *predestined* us to adoption as sons by Jesus Christ to Himself, according to the good pleasure of His will" (Ephesians 1:4-5).

We are *chosen.* God chose *us* before we chose *Him.* He chose us and saved us because of His love for us and His kindness toward us. We are *holy* because Jesus cleansed us from all sin. We are *predestined,* which does not mean we have a fatalistic look at the future, as if we are destined to be poor or miserable. It means God has a plan for our lives, and because we have received Jesus and have His Holy Spirit in us, we are now destined to live out that plan. We are *forgiven* because Jesus loved us enough to die the death we should have died and pay the price we should have paid for our sins. We have been justified, which means that now, regarding our sins, it's "just-as-if-I'd" never done it. We are *accepted* by God because we accepted Jesus and are now "in Christ" and His Spirit is in us. When God looks at us, He sees the righteousness of Jesus. And that is a beautiful thing.

Your Commander Saves You

We cannot save ourselves. Only Jesus can. Without Him we are lost. "Nor is there salvation in any other, for *there is no other name under heaven given among men by which we must be saved*" (Acts 4:12).

Anyone can be saved who calls on Jesus' name for that purpose. Paul said, "*Whoever calls on the name of the LORD shall be saved*" (Romans 10:13). He said, "*If you confess with your mouth the Lord Jesus and believe in your heart that God has raised Him from the dead, you will be saved*" (Romans 10:9). Believing with our heart and confessing with our mouth that Jesus is Lord and Savior confirms it.

If you have never established a personal relationship with Jesus, know that He has chosen you already. He waits every day for you to choose Him. You can do that by asking Him to come into your heart and forgive you of all your sins and mistakes of the past. Tell Him you want to receive Him and all He has for you. Thank Him for laying down His life for you so that you can have life with Him for all eternity and a better life now.

Everything secure in our life as a believer depends on the death and resurrection of Jesus. Without that—if Jesus had not paid the price for our sins with His death in place of ours—then we are not forgiven and saved from our own demise. *If Christ has not risen, then our faith is empty and futile because we are still dead in our sins* (1 Corinthians 15:14,17). Our faith would be a lie, a joke, a powerless fantasy. But He *did die*. And He *did rise again*. And He was seen by many on earth before He ascended into heaven.

After Jesus was crucified, the Jewish religious leaders were questioning Peter and John about what they were saying about Him. They commanded the two apostles not to speak about Jesus at all, but they refused saying, "We cannot but speak the things which we have seen and heard" (Acts 4:20). I guarantee you will be the same way because the more you know of Jesus, the less you can keep it to yourself. When you understand all He has saved you *from*, and all He has saved you *for*, you won't be able to stop talking about Him.

Allow yourself to be possessed by God by receiving Jesus, and you will never be possessed by anything else.

Your Commander Makes You a Joint Heir with Him

When you receive the Lord, you are a son or daughter of God. That makes you a brother or sister to Jesus and therefore a coheir with Him. What Jesus inherits, you will inherit too. "God sent forth His Son" to redeem us, and now we are not slaves to sin but we are sons and daughters of God, making each of us "*an heir of God through Christ*" (Galatians 4:4,7). This is no small thing, so don't ever let this truth be minimized in your life. Only a joint heir with Christ can be a prayer warrior.

Being a prayer warrior is a way of life. It is not a hit-and-miss, now-and-then, or whenever-I-feel-like-it kind of thing. Nor is it burdensome. When Jesus says, "Follow Me," He is saying, "Come out of the world and into the kingdom of God." "Come out of danger and into safety." "Come out of the darkness and into the light." "Come out of stress and into peace." He says, "Come to Me, all you who labor and are heavy laden, and I will give you rest. Take My yoke upon you and learn from Me, for I am gentle and lowly in heart, and you will find rest for your souls. *For My yoke is easy and My burden is light*" (Matthew 11:28-30). The burdens you have in your heart are laid upon Him as you pray about them. The things He wants you to do for Him are easy because *He* does the heavy lifting. This is just the beginning of receiving your inheritance.

Your Commander Gives You His Spirit to Live in You

Jesus is not here in person on earth with us because He sits at the right hand of the Father in heaven (Hebrews 1:3). From the right hand of the Father is where Jesus intercedes for us and dispenses blessings upon us.

Jesus told His disciples that when He went to the Father after He was crucified and had risen again, He would send His Holy Spirit to be *with* us and *in* us. That means when you receive Jesus, He gives you His Spirit to dwell in you. It is the sign that you belong to Him. *"You are not in the flesh but in the Spirit, if indeed the Spirit of God dwells in you. Now if anyone does not have the Spirit of Christ, he is not His" (Romans 8:9).*

This Scripture means that if you don't have His Spirit in you, you have not received Him. I am not talking about other outpourings or manifestations of the Spirit. That is another book entirely. I am talking about what happens when you receive the Lord.

When you received Jesus, *"you were sealed with the Holy Spirit of promise"* (Ephesians 1:13). The Holy Spirit in us is *"the guarantee of our inheritance,"* which means our inheritance from God is a done deal (Ephesians 1:14). This means God possesses us entirely and forever.

The Spirit of Christ—who is the Holy Spirit of God living in you—is the *power* of *God.* God shares His power with you. That is the way He gives you power over the enemy. The Bible says, "The message of the cross is foolishness to those who are perishing, but *to us who are being saved it is the power of God"* (1 Corinthians 1:18). Christ's work on the cross is the ground on which we are saved. The resurrection of Jesus was always God's plan, and it destroyed the enemy's plans and all of his power. That means *Jesus* rules in your life and the evil one does not.

When you receive the Lord, you are transported into a new kingdom, and you don't ever have to live in the realm of darkness again. Jesus said, "*I have come as a light into the world,* that whoever believes in Me should not abide in darkness" (John 12:46). We are not only going to spend eternity with Him, but we are going to reign with Him in this life as well. This all happens by the power of the Holy Spirit in us. Jesus is "not weak toward you, but mighty in you" (2 Corinthians 13:3).

By receiving Jesus you establish a living relationship with Him, and His Spirit lives in you. That is how He communicates with you. When your heart is open to what He wants to communicate to you, listen for His direction. When you hear His call to pray and are committed to answering that call, you are a prayer warrior in His great army on earth.

Your Commander Wants You to Choose His Side

We became part of the war between God and the evil one the minute we received Jesus and were declared a legal citizen of God's kingdom on earth. In this war we are either on God's side or the enemy's side. We are either in the army of God or in the forces of God's enemy. The battle lines were drawn thousands of years ago. (More about that in chapter 3, "Recognize Who Your True Enemy Is.") Everyone has to make the decision as to which side they are on. Thinking you can stay neutral—neither choosing God's side nor acknowledging the enemy—puts you on the enemy's side.

That's how some people choose the side of evil unwittingly, thinking they don't have to make that decision and can stay out of it. Some people *believe* they are choosing the right side because the enemy is able to entice the uninformed into thinking that *he* is god. But when we walk with the true God—living with His Word in our hearts and following the leading of His Holy Spirit in us—we will be able to recognize an imposter.

The more you know your Commander, the more certain you will be about whose side you are standing on. That's because to stand with any other would be unthinkable.

Being a prayer warrior is something you do because you love the

Lord and want to serve Him. As prayer warriors we now become "ambassadors for Christ" (2 Corinthians 5:20). The love of Jesus for us gives us no other choice but to live to please Him. "The love of Christ compels us" (2 Corinthians 5:14). We can only choose the winning side.

Your Commander Already Defeated the Enemy

Your Commander is the only one who has ever defeated the enemy for you. And He calls you to fight with every possible advantage—including impenetrable armor and the most powerful weapons of all. That's why we don't have to be afraid of evil powers. Jesus has completely neutralized them. Through the cross Jesus destroyed the rule on earth of principalities and powers of evil (Colossians 2:15). He did not destroy *them*, but He *did* destroy their *power* to torment those who have His Holy Spirit in them.

The enemy only has power in our lives if we allow him to. People who are influenced by the enemy are those who have given him a place in their lives, either deliberately or out of ignorance. Jesus is Lord, and we can't water that down in our hearts, nor can we compromise on that fact in our minds. *Our Commander dwells in us by His Spirit, and we must never submit to any other.* Spend time with your Leader so He can give you the strength and protection you need to stand on His side in the battle. Don't forget for a moment that God is bigger and more powerful than the enemy (1 John 4:4). Jesus has won this war. And because you are fighting on His side, you are a winner too.

Your Commander Is the Greatest Example of a Prayer Warrior

Jesus is our best role model when it comes to understanding what it means to be a prayer warrior. He not only taught about prayer; He lived it every day of His life. He prayed all the time. He did nothing without praying first. He faced the enemy often and ruled over him.

Jesus' private time with His heavenly Father was what empowered Him to do all that He did.

His disciples noticed that when Jesus went apart from them to pray, He came back empowered to do miracles. They made that connection between power and prayer. They didn't ask Him how to get the power; they asked Him to teach them how to pray. And Jesus taught them to pray what we now call the Lord's Prayer (Matthew 6:9-13).

In that prayer Jesus taught us to acknowledge God as our *heavenly Father*—which establishes our personal relationship with Him as His children. We are to enter His presence in worship, and praise Him as holy. We pray for His will to be done and His kingdom to be established on earth the way it is in heaven—which means we pray that it will be established in ourselves, in the people we love and care about, and in the world we live in.

He also taught us to pray that all our needs would be met by Him, and that God would forgive our sins in the same way we forgive others who sin against us. This puts a convicting light on any lack of forgiveness we may harbor in our heart. We are also to ask God for the strength to withstand every temptation and be *delivered from the evil one.* Lastly, we are to declare His kingdom and glory are forever.

Jesus' name was not used in this prayer because He had not yet been crucified on the cross and resurrected. When He was telling His disciples about His coming death, He said He was going to prepare a place in heaven for all who trusted in Him. He said, "*He who believes in Me, the works that I do he will do also*; and greater works than these he will do, because I go to My Father. And whatever you ask in My name, that I will do, that the Father may be glorified in the Son. *If you ask anything in My name, I will do it*" (John 14:12-14). That means because we have received Jesus, we can accomplish things *He* has done when we pray in *His* name.

Jesus' desire was always to do His heavenly Father's will and glorify Him. We must have that same desire in our hearts in order to
be the prayer warriors God is calling us to be. We must be dedicated
to communing with our heavenly Father and fulfilling His assignment to establish His kingdom in prayer here and now.

We must recognize that we have the mind of Christ and refuse to
be led by our own fleshly desires. We must not let the enemy bully
us into doing things we know are wrong and then suffering the consequences because of it. Let's not allow the enemy to keep us from
doing the right things out of fear of man, neglect, or laziness. Let us
not get *hung up* on legalism instead of getting *swept up* with Jesus
and what He accomplished on the cross. For if we do, that will limit
what God wants to do *in* and *through* us.

Because of Jesus we have a direct connection to God. By receiving Him we are receiving His kingdom that cannot be moved. There
is severe punishment for those who throw away the revelation they
have of Jesus. When Jesus returns all that is earthly and temporary
will be gone and only that which is eternal and of God will remain.
We are receiving an *unshakeable kingdom* so that we can serve God
without fear (Hebrews 12:25-29). Welcome to the kingdom of God.

If you have received Christ as Savior, the enemy's power in your
life has been annihilated. Unless the enemy can convince you to
doubt God's Word and all that Jesus accomplished, the enemy has
no power. Instead of listening to the enemy, hold fast to God speaking to you through His Word and through His Holy Spirit in you,
and you will have power over the enemy for the rest of your life.

Prayer for the Prayer Warrior

Lord, by You the world was created and all things on earth and in heaven. Everything comes from You and consists in You. Thank You, Lord, that You hold the world together. Thank You, Jesus, for saving me, forgiving me, and freeing me from the mortal wounds my sins have inflicted on me. Thank You, Lord, that You never change. You are "the same yesterday, today, and forever" (Hebrews 13:8). Help me to imitate You in all things. Keep me from following anything that is not of You (Hebrews 13:9).

Thank You, Jesus, for the inheritance You have secured for me—both in this life and in the life to come. Thank You for the great hope I have in You. Thank You for choosing me even before I chose You. Thank You that You protect me from the enemy when I live Your way and pray according to Your will as You have taught me in Your Word. Thank You that because I have put my faith in You, I have received Your Holy Spirit and this seals my future of spending eternity with You. I praise You for paying the price to win the war against the enemy of my soul.

I choose to stand on Your side in this war between good and evil. Teach me how to be the powerful prayer warrior You have called me to be. Enable me to take dominion over the works of darkness and take back territory the enemy has stolen from me and the rest of Your people. Help me to stand strong in prayer against the encroachment of the enemy into my life, as well as the lives of others. Enable me to serve You, being led by Your Holy Spirit in prayer. Thank You, Lord, that You will protect me and those for whom I pray. Thank You for sharing Your power with me as I pray in Your name so that I can win each battle and defeat the enemy.

In Jesus' name I pray.

When the whirlwind passes by,
the wicked is no more,
but the righteous has an everlasting foundation.

PROVERBS 10:25

3

RECOGNIZE WHO
YOUR TRUE ENEMY IS

Winning a war doesn't happen automatically. You have to first of all clearly identify who you are fighting and why.

This is what we know about our enemy. He is a created being—an angel—who was in heaven with God. His name was Lucifer, which means "son of the morning." "How you are fallen from heaven, O Lucifer, son of the morning! How you are cut down to the ground, you who weakened the nations!" (Isaiah 14:12). Lucifer was the leader of all the angels and ranked highest among them. He was beautiful and bright, and his pride led him to attempt to take over rulership from God. "You have said in your heart: 'I will ascend into heaven, I will exalt my throne above the stars of God'" (Isaiah 14:13). He wanted to *be* God, so he rebelled against God. His arrogance caused him to try and take control of heaven from God.

When the battle for God's throne happened, Lucifer and one third of the angels who rebelled with him fell from heaven to earth. Then he was "called the Devil and Satan, who deceives the whole world; he was cast to the earth, and his angels were cast out with him" (Revelation 12:9).

On earth Satan became a master of disguise and his angels became evil spirits. "Satan himself transforms himself into an angel of light" (2 Corinthians 11:14). He is the author of lies and operates by deception. He and his evil spirits work against those of us who are not on his side by continually attempting to draw us away from God and His truth and all God has for us.

Don't think for a moment that to understand some things about Satan and his evil forces is going to open up that world to you. It's already all around you. Some Christians mistakenly believe that if they ignore the realm of the enemy it will all go away. Far from it! The realm of the enemy is only operating because we believers are not in the battle to stop it. The enemy and his minions are always walking around looking for whom they can oppress. We don't have to do business with evil; we have to follow the Lord Jesus—our Commander—and be about our *heavenly Father's* business.

The Truth About Who the Enemy Is

Good soldiers know that if they don't recognize who their enemy is, they are destined to lose the war. That is also true for those of us who do battle in God's army. Even though Jesus put the enemy under His feet and won the victory for us, we still must move into that victory. There are still battles to be fought in prayer.

In World War I and World War II when the war was won and the enemy was defeated, there were still pockets of enemy fighters who refused to give up. They would attack from out of the darkness where they were hidden. They kept fighting a war they had already lost as long as they possibly could. Too many times our spiritual enemy attacks us and succeeds just because he can. He knows that far too many people will not oppose him because they either don't know he is there or don't recognize his character, the way he operates, and that the war is still going on.

One of my family members is in the military, and he says every soldier has to know the weaknesses and strengths of his enemy. He doesn't have to be personally acquainted with the enemy; he just has to know the way the enemy works and what his tactics are. We, too, must be able to identify who our enemy is and what he *is* and *is not* capable of doing. We must know the way he operates so we can identify any attempt he makes to influence our life or the lives of others.

An accurate profile of our enemy—God's enemy—is on record in the Bible. Jesus, Paul, John, Matthew, and David were quoted about the spiritual forces of evil and how we should respond to them. The Lord and these godly men wanted us to be fully aware of who our enemy is. Below are some of the enemy's names they mentioned so we can identify his character whenever we see it manifesting in a person or situation. The enemy is:

The father of lies. "He was a murderer from the beginning, and does not stand in the truth, because there is no truth in him. When he speaks a lie, he speaks from his own resources, for he is a liar and the father of it" (John 8:44).

The thief. "The thief does not come except to steal, and to kill, and to destroy. I have come that they may have life, and that they may have it more abundantly" (John 10:10).

The great dragon and serpent. "The great dragon was cast out, that serpent of old, called the Devil and Satan, who deceives the whole world; he was cast to the earth, and his angels were cast out with him" (Revelation 12:9).

The tempter. "When the tempter came to Him, he said, 'If You are the Son of God, command that these stones become bread'" (Matthew 4:3).

The enemy and the avenger. "Out of the mouth of babes and nursing infants you have ordained strength, because of Your enemies, that You may silence the enemy and the avenger" (Psalm 8:2).

The accuser. "I heard a loud voice saying in heaven, 'Now salvation, and strength, and the kingdom of our God, and the power of His Christ have come, for the accuser of our brethren, who accused them before our God day and night, has been cast down'" (Revelation 12:10).

The evil one. "Do not lead us into temptation, but deliver us from the evil one. For Yours is the kingdom and the power and the glory forever" (Matthew 6:13).

The adversary. "Be sober, be vigilant; because your adversary the devil walks about like a roaring lion, seeking whom he may devour" (1 Peter 5:8).

The ruler of this world. "I will no longer talk much with you, for the ruler of this world is coming, and he has nothing in Me" (John 14:30).

The prince of the power of the air. "You He made alive, who were dead in trespasses and sins, in which you once walked according to the course of this world, according to the prince of the power of the air, the spirit who now works in the sons of disobedience" (Ephesians 2:1-2).

The reason to know all this is to be able to put the blame for certain things that happen exactly where it belongs. We must never blame God for what the enemy does. The enemy is the one who steals and kills, not God. The enemy is our adversary, accuser, tempter, and father of lies, not God. The enemy wants to destroy the life God has for us. We must recognize these things if we want to successfully stand against *God's* enemy and ours.

The Truth About the Enemy's Lies

The enemy and his evil spirits cannot possess a believer, but they can try to oppress us with lies about who Jesus is, who God is, and who we are in Christ. The enemy can attempt to confuse us or draw us into anger, anxiety, bitterness, despair, and fear. I am not saying we can't get into those conditions on our own. We can. But the enemy is always trying to lure us into believing or feeling *opposite* of what God wants us to believe or feel. The enemy accomplishes that by getting us to accept *his lies* as truth. Because God has given us a free will, we can put a stop to the enemy's lies by *choosing* to believe God instead.

One of the main ways the enemy draws people away from God is through deception. I know of a pastor's wife in a church I spoke at many years ago who told me she never said the enemy's name or mentioned him and she never read any passage in the Bible that contained anything about him. She didn't want him to notice her or her family, and so by not acknowledging the enemy she felt she wouldn't attract his attention. I could not believe how absolutely opposite that was to the truth in the Bible and Jesus' own words. I don't know if her husband believed the same thing or not, but I can only assume so. As it turned out, their daughter's life was ruined in a horrible car accident, and their son had such disagreements with his parents that the family was split apart. Their church dwindled so much that the pastor eventually lost his pastorate completely. No enemy? Really? We can certainly see how well denying the enemy's existence worked for them.

Denying the enemy's existence to the point of not even reading any Scripture in the Bible referring to him puts a person right where the enemy wants them—CLUELESS! It is one of his greatest deceptions of all. And pastors along with their families are *prime* targets. The enemy aims for them, and that's why we prayer warriors must pray for our pastors and their families so that no weapon formed against them *by the enemy* will prosper.

Everyone who believes in Jesus is the enemy's target. *God's* enemy will always be *our* enemy. No amount of denying he exists will change that. One of my beloved pastors, Pastor Rice, said, "With every step you take away from God, there will be someone there telling you that you are doing the right thing." That's why we must study God's Word so we don't end up clueless about who our enemy is. We must be able to discern between the truth and a lie.

Those who stick their head in the sand regarding the enemy and spiritual warfare are bound to get kicked in the most obvious part of their anatomy still exposed.

Don't be deceived by the enemy's angel-of-light routine. Ask the

Spirit of truth within you to keep you *undeceived*. Because if you don't, you are surely headed for a painful experience.

The Enemy's First Deception

In the Garden of Eden, the enemy came to Eve in the form of a serpent. He fed her lies, giving her ideas that were contrary to what God had told her and Adam. He contradicted God's Word and enticed her to eat the only fruit forbidden by God. She protested, saying that God told her anyone eating this fruit would die. The serpent lied to the woman, saying, "'You will not surely die. For God knows that in the day you eat of it your eyes will be opened, and you will be like God, knowing good and evil.' So when the woman saw that the tree was good for food, that it was pleasant to the eyes, and a tree desirable to make one wise, she took of its fruit and ate. She also gave to her husband with her, and he ate" (Genesis 3:4-6). The enemy caused her to question God's Word and she fell for it.

When Adam and Eve disobeyed God, they were cast out of the garden, where they had enjoyed a close relationship with the Lord and a perfect life. And man has been trying to get close to God and find the perfect life ever since.

We're beginning to see a pattern here. Rebelling against God and disobeying His rules doesn't have good results. Anyone doing so gets cast out from all God has for them. Even though Eve was *deceived* by the enemy, and Adam *chose* to disobey, the results were the same. Disaster.

The enemy takes the same approach with us, attempting to make us doubt what God has said. He tells us, "Go ahead and do it." "No one will know." "You deserve this." "God didn't really say that." "God doesn't actually care about you." And a person not grounded in the Word will think they are hearing revelation from God. That's why we must know the Word of God extremely well. The Word of God is how Jesus dealt with Satan when he came to tempt Him in the wilderness. We must deal with the enemy's attack on our lives the same way.

The enemy will always come to try to entice you to doubt God. He will tempt you to be dissatisfied with what God has given you. He will cause you to question what God is doing or has called you to do. That's why you have to know with certainty who God is, what Jesus accomplished, and who you are in the Lord. When you hear something like, "It's okay to do that because *everyone is doing it*," stand strong in God's Word and in prayer and refuse to buy into his lies.

Adam and Eve only had to be concerned with *one* commandment of the Lord to them. There wasn't a lot of memorization involved, but perhaps there should have been. It wasn't that Adam and Eve didn't know what God had instructed them to not do; they just listened to the wrong voice telling them it was okay not to do it. That voice was the enemy speaking through your average friendly talking snake.

Let this be a lesson. Don't accept input from anyone who opposes the Word of God, no matter how cute and cuddly they are.

This struggle between Eve and the enemy is the first battle recorded in the Word. The problem was she didn't realize the snake was her enemy. She thought he was a friend. She believed him over God. How often are people influenced by something someone says who has charm, a nice smile, the appearance of caring about them, and a persuasive way? *Way too often!* We have to keep our eyes wide open to the truth. We have to cling to God and His Word and resist anyone who opposes it.

Your primary battle will always be with the enemy who wants to impose his will on your life and stop God's plan for you from succeeding. Every step of disobedience to God's ways puts you in collusion with the enemy. You don't even have to commit some heinous crime. All gossip, envy, unkindness, rudeness, cruelty, or impure thoughts puts us in a working relationship with the enemy while grieving the Holy Spirit in us.

Our war is always with the enemy of our souls, and we must win it. And we *will* win it by staying close to God and His Word and seeking to be led by His Holy Spirit in all things. Each battle is ours to lose by resisting God and His ways. We are joint heirs with Christ and will inherit all His victories, but we still have to live His way in order to receive that full inheritance.

Pray that you will never fall into deception. The apostle Paul said, "I fear, lest somehow, as the serpent deceived Eve by his craftiness, so *your minds may be corrupted from the simplicity that is in Christ*" (2 Corinthians 11:3). The gospel message is simple. Beware of those who make it complicated by their confusing doctrine that calls everything in the Word into question. The apostle Paul was concerned that people would listen to deceptive voices and begin to doubt everything. He said, "If he who comes preaches another Jesus whom we have not preached, or if you receive a different spirit which you have not received, or a different gospel which you have not accepted—you may well put up with it!" (2 Corinthians 11:4). You can get accustomed to the voices of doubt and start doubting *God's* voice.

RUN, DON'T WALK, away from any voice that tells you it is okay to disobey God's commandments and His personal instructions to you.

In a weak moment you may have doubt and fall for the enemy's lies, but the point is to not let there be any weak moments. Fortify yourself in God's Word, in prayer, and in worship and praise. I'm certain Eve regretted falling for the enemy's deception, and Adam kicked himself for his bad choice. They became the first ones to prove that you truly never know what you have until it's gone.

The Enemy Wants to Destroy Your Family

The second battle recorded in the Bible—after the enemy's attack on Adam and Eve—also occurred within a family. Often our greatest battles involve keeping family relationships strong. The struggles between siblings, parents, children, husband and wife, or any other family relationship is age old. And who do you think would be most pleased with the dissolution of our family relationships? The enemy, of course. Unfortunately, far too many people don't understand that. They play right into his hand by being unloving, cruel, selfish, and inconsiderate to their family members and allowing family bonds to be destroyed just because they think they have the right to do so. This battle for our family is one we must win. Losing this battle causes too many casualties.

This first family battle in the Bible was between two brothers. One brother, Abel, did the right thing and worshipped God the way God asked him to. The other brother, Cain, did not. Because of that, Abel had God's approval and Cain didn't. Cain became jealous of Abel and the favor he had with God, and Cain thought that the only way to solve the problem was to murder his brother.

God asked Cain why he was angry at Abel when he knew that if he did the right thing he would have favor with God too. God said to Cain, "If you do not do well, sin lies at the door. And its desire is for you, but you should rule over it" (Genesis 4:7). We have to remember that sin waits at the door for all of us. The enemy is continually setting traps to trip us up by enticing us to disobey God. But we *have a choice. We can rule over it.* Cain did *not* rule over his enticement to sin, so his punishment was severe and affected his entire family. It is the same for us. When we have a difficult family member, we must not go to battle against *him* or *her*. We must go to God and pray for that person to come to a knowledge of God's truth.

For example, jealousy has always been satanic at its source. Lucifer was jealous of God, and it was his downfall. We will never become all we were created to be if we allow jealousy to reside in us. If you are jealous of someone, reject the enemy's influence, confess that before God, and ask for a change of heart. If someone is jealous of *you*, pray that God will break that stronghold and open blind eyes to the truth of God's powerful love that brings healing, restoration, and countless blessings.

Don't let the enemy win the war for your family. Just because people become influenced by the enemy and may act like the devil, your true enemy is the evil one. The enemy works through other people who often don't even know they are being used. He entices them through their own evil desires and they do his bidding. If your family is fractured in any way, know that this is not God's will. It is the enemy's plan. If the destruction of important family relationships has already happened to you, pray for the people involved to see the enemy's hand in this and resist him by turning to God. If they refuse, release them into God's hands. He has far more effective tools of persuasion than you do.

The Enemy Wants Sin to Reign in Our Lives

As Jesus was about to be arrested and sentenced to die, He said to His disciples, "I will no longer talk much with you, *for the ruler of this world is coming, and he has nothing in Me*" (John 14:30). Satan had nothing in Jesus because Jesus was sinless. That proves that the enemy can have something *in us* if we give him a place in our mind, emotions, attitude, or will. If we compromise on living God's way, the enemy can gain a foothold in our life. He cannot possess us because the Spirit of God is in us and *He* possesses us, but the enemy can cause us to lose our footing and fall off the path God has for us. He can delay the blessings God waits to give us until we come to our senses and return fully to Him. Don't align yourself with the enemy by allowing sin to stay in your life.

When predicting His death on the cross, Jesus said, "Now the ruler of this world will be cast out. And I, if I am lifted up from the earth, will draw all peoples to Myself" (John 12:31-32). What Jesus accomplished on the cross defeated the enemy. And the enemy cannot stop us from lifting up Jesus in our heart.

In another example of the enemy's deception, the apostle Peter confronted a man named Ananias regarding his holding back money from land he sold that he had vowed to give to the Lord. Peter said, "Ananias, *why has Satan filled your heart to lie to the Holy Spirit* and keep back part of the price of the land for yourself? While it remained, was it not your own? And after it was sold, was it not in your own control? Why have you conceived this thing in your heart? *You have not lied to men but to God*" (Acts 5:3-4).

Satan had put deception in Ananias' heart, and he sinned by lying to the apostles and therefore to God. The result was that Ananias died suddenly. All it takes is what seems like a little sin for it to turn into major consequences.

I receive a shipment every few months of a certain food supplement with vitamins. It comes in protective shrink-wrap made of clear plastic that is impenetrable by human hands. There is no way anyone is going to break that seal without some kind of sharp instrument. Believe me, I have tried. But I have found that if I can make even the tiniest hole in it with the smallest needle, I have won the battle. That tiny opening weakens the entire package enough that I can completely destroy the protective barrier.

That's what happens when we entertain even the tiniest sin in our lives. (Actually, I don't think God looks at any sin as tiny.) All it takes is allowing the enemy to gain even the slightest opening into our heart through sin, and he can gain a foot in the door of our lives. Though the enemy *cannot* penetrate the protective blood barrier of Christ, he *can* gain access to our heart and mind if we allow what we might think is the smallest sin in without confession and repentance before God.

We want to be able to say as Jesus did that "the ruler of this world has nothing in me." The enemy can only have an inroad into our life if we give him an opening. Paul instructed us not to "give place to the devil" (Ephesians 4:27). The way we give place to the devil is by disobeying God in any way. By making an idol out of something the enemy dangles in front of us. By not walking away from temptation the first moment we are presented with it. The culture that tries to suppress God by holding back information about Him is destined to be destroyed. Evil rises as the knowledge of God decreases.

Jesus "gave Himself for our sins, that *He might deliver us from this present evil age,* according to the will of our God and Father" (Galatians 1:4). This present evil age is dominated by the enemy of God, but Jesus has rescued us who believe in Him from all the enemy's power. When we receive Jesus into our hearts, we are out from under the domination of the enemy and this present evil age. This means we are delivered from everything that separates us from God and keeps us from moving into all He has for us.

Concentrate on the Goodness of God, Not the Work of the Enemy

Don't attempt to understand all of the evil things the enemy does outside of what the Bible tells you. You don't need to. You are instructed to "be wise in what is good, and simple concerning evil. And *the God of peace will crush Satan under your feet shortly*" (Romans 16:19-20). You have to know who your enemy is and what is his intent, but you don't need to dwell on his evil deeds except as the Holy Spirit makes you aware of something for which He wants you to pray. That doesn't mean do nothing. Too many people think, *I don't have to do anything because God will take care of everything for me.* This is not true. God gives us a free will, and we are judged by what we choose to do in response to what God says. God has mandated that we pray. Fervently! Without ceasing! Don't think that the enemy can't win some battles if we don't do what God instructs us to do. He *can* and he *will.* Too many believers have been deceived by the enemy into thinking they don't need to pray or that their prayers are powerless.

God has given us a choice. He has set it up that we have a will, and we decide what we *will* or *will not* do. Will we or will we *not* worship God? Will we or will we *not* use God's Word as our spiritual weapon against the realm of darkness? *We* decide. When we align *our will* with *God's will*, that's when we see the enemy pushed back. The enemy wants to keep that from happening, of course. He wants to distract you, deceive you, discourage you, and destroy you so that God's purposes for your life will never be fulfilled.

Does it ever seem as though something is always coming along to defeat you? If so, it is likely the enemy trying to wear you down and get you off the path of fulfilling God's plan for your life. Remember that if you lose your job, or get sick, or an important relationship suddenly disintegrates, or your world seems to be caving in for whatever reason, God is still on the throne. You may be devastated, but He is not. He still sees His high purpose for you and His plan for your life, even if you cannot see it at that moment. You have a good future, but it doesn't happen by chance. You have an enemy who wants to steal your future away. Don't allow that to happen. Become the prayer warrior God is calling you to be and fight for it.

Look what has happened in our schools, workplaces, neighborhoods, marriages, children, finances, and governments. The enemy has moved in on them while we were sleeping or changing channels, and he has erected major strongholds around us. Don't allow the enemy to have one more inch of ground. Do not "give place to the devil" in any way, not even by your own inaction (Ephesians 4:27). Focus on God and what He is calling you to do as His prayer warrior.

The Enemy May Appear Strong, but Only God Is All-Powerful

The enemy's power is limited, but God's power is without limit. The enemy is not all-powerful. Only God is. The only way the enemy has power is because people give it to him. People give it to him because he makes them think he doesn't exist. Don't dwell on how strong the enemy can be. Dwell on the all-powerful strength of the Lord, for whom nothing is impossible. The enemy's power is limited by what we will allow him to do. The Lord's power has no limits except when we limit His access to our lives.

In response to those who don't believe the devil exists, why then did Jesus come to destroy the works of the devil? Why did Jesus say, "The Spirit of the LORD is upon Me, because He has anointed Me to preach the gospel to the poor; He has sent Me to heal the brokenhearted, *to proclaim liberty to the captives* and recovery of sight to the blind, *to set at liberty those who are oppressed*" (Luke 4:18)? Jesus destroyed the devil's power, but he is still here. And will be here until the time appointed by God for his destruction.

Stay under the umbrella of God's protection, which has been secured by the blood of Jesus. Just as the blood of a lamb over the doorpost of the Israelites in Egypt protected them when the Lord passed over them to kill every firstborn child of the Egyptians, so too the blood of Jesus over you is powerful to protect you from the plans of the enemy.

The enemy wants to destroy your mind, health, marriage, relationships, children, finances, hope, and the inheritance you have in Christ. The Bible says, "*Be sober, be vigilant; because your adversary the devil walks about like a roaring lion, seeking whom he may devour*" (1 Peter 5:8). You must prepare for his attempts to devour your life by being vigilant as a prayer warrior. We are instructed to take God's kingdom by force because that is the only way to take it from an enemy who is opposing us every step of the way. The enemy comes to tempt us away from God's best for our lives. But God protects us when we turn to Him.

The enemy is not everywhere. He can only be where there is an opening for him. The enemy does not know everything, and he does not know what you think. He only knows what you *say*. So watch what you say. If you say, "I hate my life and I don't want to live anymore," the enemy will help you get what you say you want. If you say, "I can do all things through Christ who strengthens me" or "Praise You, Jesus. I worship You as Lord and Savior, Deliverer and Redeemer," the enemy is powerless and can do nothing. The enemy is not even close to being as powerful as God. Only God is all-powerful.

People Who Reject God's Truth Will Be Given Over to a Spirit of Deception

People are given a choice when they hear God's truth. And those who do not receive the truth will be given over to strong delusion. "The coming of the lawless one is according to the working of Satan, with all power, signs, and lying wonders, and with all unrighteous deception among those who perish, *because they did not receive the love of the truth, that they might be saved.* And for this reason *God will send them strong delusion, that they should believe the lie,* that they all may be condemned who did not believe the truth but had pleasure in unrighteousness" (2 Thessalonians 2:9-12).

This is serious.

This means the enemy will be able to seriously and *continually* deceive anyone who rejects the truth. "The Spirit expressly says that in latter times some will depart from the faith, *giving heed to deceiving spirits and doctrines of demons,* speaking lies in hypocrisy, having their own conscience seared with a hot iron" (1 Timothy 4:1-2). We see this all the time.

Do you ever wonder how *you* can see God's truth so clearly regarding something and there are those who cannot see it at all? It happens because at some point in time they *chose* to reject God's truth and believe a lie. So they were given over to the deception of the enemy. This is not just a temporary condition until they come to their senses. This is a major stronghold that would take major deliverance by the Deliverer requiring great repentance and awakening on the part of the deceived.

Before I came to the Lord, I was searching into a number of occult practices and religions, trying to find a way to God. One of those supposed ways was a religion that believed there was no such thing as evil in the world. Evil only existed in your mind. So if you got rid of all evil in your mind, there would be no evil in your life. Right! We can clearly see how well that works. It was a very big religion in Hollywood at the time that used Christian terms to mean something different. Who do you think was the author of that religion? Yes, the deceiver himself. If he can get us to believe that, then he can accomplish anything he wants through us and make us think it's a good idea. What a great deception by him. That religion had a lot of success until the high-profile Manson murders at that time in Los Angeles. They were so shocking that people had a hard time believing that the unthinkable slaughter of seven innocent victims was all in their mind. The spirit of evil was palpable and people had a hard time denying it.

When I came to know the Lord and was finally able to see evil for what it is, it was *liberating*. When I understood for the first time that Jesus destroyed the power of the enemy, it was *empowering*.

You must know who your enemy is. You cannot be a prayer *warrior* if you don't believe there is, or ever *will* be, a battle. If you don't think you have an enemy, you have been blinded to his existence exactly according to his plan. You have the power to choose the light or the darkness. Those who choose the wrong path will never know God.

Yes, people can give place to an evil spirit in their lives and be deceived enough by it to do its bidding, and so evil things happen. But the eternal future of those people who do such things without repentance before God is a lifetime of total separation from Him. Some people don't realize that everything good in this world happens because of the goodness of God. Separation from God is not going to be as much fun as they think.

The enemy of our soul will try to oppress us. He will afflict us with situations or conditions designed to discourage us, wear us down, steal from us, and destroy us. It may be through external situations that come upon us. We've all seen the incredible force of a flood in the news. It has a destructive power beyond what we can even imagine. When the enemy comes in with that kind of destructive magnitude in our lives, the power of the Lord will raise up a barrier against him so that the enemy is powerless and can do nothing. "When the enemy comes in like a flood, the Spirit of the LORD will lift up a standard against him" (Isaiah 59:19). Praise be to God for that! "The Lord is faithful, who will establish you and guard you from the evil one" (2 Thessalonians 3:3).

Everything God rules is good and pure. Everything the enemy rules is corrupt. When you see people hating one another, lying to one another, mistreating one another, or enslaving each other, you can know for certain the enemy is in charge. When you see people starving, homeless, or mistreated with no one to help, you know the enemy is in charge. When you see helpless people slaughtered, destroyed by disease, persecuted, riddled with war, you know the enemy is in charge. This all happens when people reject God's truth and allow the enemy's lies to rule.

Our prayers can change that.

We are all related—every believer. "He has made *from one blood* every nation of men to dwell on all the face of the earth, and has determined their preappointed times and the boundaries of their dwellings" (Acts 17:26). God cares for *everyone*—even the worst of people. We should pray for our human enemies to be brought to their knees in repentance before God. It is up to God as to whether He will answer that prayer or not.

Adam and Eve had dominion over the earth, but they lost that privilege when they were duped by the enemy into disobeying God. But because of Jesus, God has once again given us dominion on earth. "The heaven, even the heavens, are the LORD's; but the earth He has given to the children of men" (Psalm 115:16). We are in charge, not the enemy. So we must step up and *be* in charge. And that happens when prayer warriors pray.

Prayer for the Prayer Warrior

LORD, I thank You that You have given us everything we need to stand strong against the enemy of our soul. It is You "who gives us the victory through our Lord Jesus Christ" (1 Corinthians 15:57). I acknowledge You as my Commander, and I submit myself to You as Your servant. Help me to serve You in prayer as You have asked me to do. Enable me to oppose the plans of the enemy in prayer.

Help me to always understand who my enemy is and be able to clearly recognize his hand in everything. I know You do not ever bring confusion on us, but You can confuse the enemy (1 Corinthians 14:32). Whenever he tries to cause confusion in my life, I pray You will cause confusion in his camp when I pray. I know the enemy is no match for You, and the only way he gains power is by deceiving people into believing his lies. Keep me from all deception.

Thank You, Lord, for protecting me and those I pray for from evil people who do the enemy's bidding. Thank You, Jesus, that we can be delivered from "unreasonable and wicked men" (2 Thessalonians 3:2). Keep me from becoming fearful when I see the wicked succeeding in their terrible plans. Enable me to rise up against the enemy in prayer as You are calling me to do.

Keep me from all sin so that I will never allow the enemy to have a wedge in my life. I want to only do what pleases You and never do the enemy's bidding. I know that only You are everywhere. The enemy is not. Only You are all-powerful and know everything. Neither of those is true of the enemy. Help me to remember these things at all times.

In Jesus' name I pray.

We do not wrestle against flesh and blood, but against principalities, against powers, against the rulers of the darkness of this age, against spiritual hosts of wickedness in the heavenly places.

EPHESIANS 6:12

4

BE CERTAIN OF
YOUR AUTHORITY IN PRAYER

One of the most important things you must be sure of as a prayer warrior is your authority in prayer. If you are not absolutely one hundred percent certain about it, the enemy will attempt to bombard you with doubt. Some of his favorite whispered words to your mind will be, "You can't pray." "God doesn't hear your prayers." "What makes you think God will listen to you?" "You have no authority because you are not good enough." "Your prayers won't get past the ceiling." "God doesn't answer *your* prayers."

These kinds of taunts are an attack strategy from the enemy, but they can be shut down in an instant when you know without any hesitation who you are in the Lord and where your authority comes from. We *all* need to know this, otherwise we will continually sit in judgment on ourselves and our prayers and eventually become defeated and give up praying at all. There is no need for that. It doesn't have to happen, ever! That's because the basis for your authority as a prayer warrior never changes.

You Have Authority Because You Have Jesus

You qualify as a prayer warrior because of what is in your heart, remember? The foundation for your authority in prayer is that you have received Jesus and have *His Spirit* in your heart. The Bible says Jesus "*is not weak toward you, but mighty in you*" (2 Corinthians 13:3).

It says of Jesus that "though He was crucified in weakness, yet He lives by the power of God. For we also are weak in Him, but we shall live with Him by the power of God toward you" (2 Corinthians 13:4).

Isn't that the best? Even though we are weak, His Spirit *in us* makes us strong.

That takes the pressure off because it's not about us. It's about *Him*. It's never about us. *Everything we have—including our ability to pray in power—comes from God.* "Not that we are sufficient of ourselves to think of anything as being from ourselves, but our sufficiency is from God" (2 Corinthians 3:5). We just have to pray as He leads us, and He does it all.

We should examine and test ourselves to see if we are in the faith, and we do that by *reading God's Word* (2 Corinthians 13:5). His Word in our hearts, and His Holy Spirit in us teaching us as we read, help us to live God's way. Unless we have disqualified ourselves with sin of some kind, we are Christ's, and we can come before God and pray in Jesus' name and *God always recognizes our authority in prayer because we are one of His kids.* We have His DNA. We are members of His family and as a result we have certain rights and privileges.

When my children were young and their father and I were in the studio recording—in other words, occupied with the family business—they knew they could call us any time and we would always take their call immediately and without hesitation. We wouldn't take the calls of others because they weren't our kids. You are one of God's kids, and He will always take your calls because of that.

The grounds for your authority in prayer as a prayer warrior are that Jesus triumphed over sin, death, hell, and all evil power when He suffered and died on the cross and rose again from the dead. Because of that, Jesus is "above all *principality, power, might,* and *dominion"* which refers to the rulers and authorities in the invisible realm (Ephesians 1:21). There is a hierarchy of evil powers that are not visible to us, and they advance their dark plans and strategies through these forces. But Jesus, whose power is far above that of the evil forces of darkness, said to the believers He sent out that He gave them authority over *"all the power of the enemy"* (Luke 10:19). That power is demonstrated when we enter into spiritual warfare, and that happens when we pray.

Remember that Jesus' shed blood and resurrection are the grounds for your authority over all evil power when you pray. You have no need of any other.

The fact that you have received Jesus means that everything He accomplished on the cross applies to you. You have been reconciled to God once and for all and sealed by the Holy Spirit *in* you. It is finished. To run in fear of the enemy is to discount what Jesus has done. I am not saying to hang out with evil people. Far from it. Avoid them for sure. But you can pray for them to be brought to their knees before God, and their evil influences to be evaporated like fog in the light of the shining sun. Every time you pray, you shine *the light of the world* on evil, and evil cannot exist in *the light of the Son.*

Jesus is the source of all your authority and power. When you receive Him, He shares both of those with you. That means you have authority and power in prayer based on what He accomplished. Don't let anyone water this down in your mind and heart. This is the basic foundation of all Christianity, and if you allow for anything other than this, you will build on a weak foundation and what you build is destined to crumble.

Build on the solid foundation that is in Christ.

It is extremely important that you are *always aware* of where your authority in prayer comes from. But not only aware of it, you must be *absolutely convinced* without a doubt. Because if you don't know for certain where your authority lies, you will either be deceived into thinking you are praying under your own power, or you will become afraid that you don't have what it takes to be a prayer warrior at all. The freedom and security of being a prayer warrior is *knowing* that only *Jesus* has what it takes.

There must be no doubt about that.

Having the proper authority is extremely important. Even Jesus did not speak on His own authority before He was crucified and resurrected from the dead. He said, "I have not spoken on My own authority; but the Father who sent Me gave Me a command, what I should say and what I should speak...whatever I speak, just as the Father has told Me, so I speak" (John 12:49-50). *We* don't pray on our own authority either, but on the authority given to us by the Lord.

This is something you must be sure of at all times, because that certainty of your authority in the spirit realm means you are instantly ready as a prayer warrior whenever the Holy Spirit prompts your heart. Keep your mind focused on the Lord and not the enemy. Jesus said, "Do not rejoice in this, that the spirits are subject to you, but rather rejoice because your names are written in heaven" (Luke 10:20).

This is extremely important.

Your name written in heaven is a record of your authority in prayer.

Take possession of what *Jesus* has taken possession of for *you*. Paul said, "I press on, that *I may lay hold of that for which Christ Jesus has also laid hold of me*" (Philippians 3:12). Laying hold of all that Jesus did helps you understand your authority in prayer.

You can't win the battles you will face if you are not convinced you have authority as a prayer warrior. And I assure you, those battles will come whether you are a prayer warrior or not. But if you *are* a prayer warrior, you can be confident that your authority is established because of what Jesus has accomplished. Below are some of the things He has done for you that you must never forget.

You Have Authority Because of the Name of Jesus

The name of Jesus alone gives you authority you cannot possibly have without legitimate identification with Him.

Not just anyone can use the name of Jesus and be heard by Him. Jesus has only given those of us who have established a relationship with Him the authority and power to use *His* name. Jesus said, *"If you ask anything in My name, I will do it"* (John 14:14). He has given you the right to use His name as authorization to take your petition before God's throne. He said, *"Whatever you ask the Father in My name He will give you. Until now you have asked nothing in My name. Ask, and you will receive, that your joy may be full"* (John 16:23-24). That is an amazing promise, and its full significance must be anchored in our minds and hearts.

Jesus' name is greater than all other names. *"God also has highly exalted Him and given Him the name which is above every name,* that at the name of Jesus every knee should bow, of those in heaven, and of those on earth, and of those under the earth, and that every tongue should confess that Jesus Christ is Lord, to the glory of God the Father"* (Philippians 2:9-11). You must have this truth etched in your heart and mind so it cannot be stolen away.

Don't minimize what Jesus did for you by questioning the authority He has given you to pray in His name.

The Bible says of you and me, "What is man that You are mindful of him, or the son of man that You take care of him? *You have made him a little lower than the angels*; You have *crowned him with glory and honor*, and *set him over the works of Your hands. You have put all things in subjection under his feet"* (Hebrews 2:6-8). Don't let the enemy lie to you about this. You now know the truth.

And what did Jesus do for us? He was "made a little lower than the angels, for the suffering of death crowned with glory and honor, that He, by the grace of God, might taste death for everyone" (Hebrews 2:9). When God raised Jesus from the dead and seated Him at His right hand above all evil powers, *His name was also elevated far above "every name that is named,* not only in this age but also in that which is to come. And He put all things under His feet" (Ephesians 1:21-22).

Now *that* is authority!

And He gives this authority in His name to you and me. We have authority in prayer as prayer warriors for Him. Don't let the enemy tell you any different. *You have the authority!*

You Have Authority Because Jesus Rescued You from the Tyranny of Evil

God has "*delivered us from the power of darkness and conveyed us into the kingdom of the Son* of His love, in whom we have redemption through His blood, the forgiveness of sins" (Colossians 1:13-14).

The word "conveyed" in terms of war has to do with an army that has been captured and sent to another place—often from one country to another. Jesus captured us from the kingdom of darkness and conveyed us to His kingdom of light. We have been transferred out of enemy territory and into God's kingdom. This adds to the authority we have been given to stand in prayer against the evil powers of darkness that want to wage war against the kingdom of God and His people and bring us back into darkness.

You have been given a place of rulership over evil. Because you have "received Christ Jesus the Lord, *so walk in Him*, rooted and built up in Him and established in the faith, as you have been taught, abounding in it with thanksgiving" (Colossians 2:6-7). The Bible says we are "*complete in Him, who is the head of all principality and power*" (Colossians 2:10). That means you have everything you need in Him.

Because Jesus has overcome the world, you can too. He said, "In the world you will have tribulation; but be of good cheer, I have overcome the world" (John 16:33).

When Jesus was asked by the Pharisees when the kingdom of God would come, He said, "The kingdom of God does not come with observation" (Luke 17:20). In other words, we won't find it by looking. The kingdom is *in* us. Jesus said, "I will give you the keys of the kingdom of heaven, and *whatever you bind on earth will be bound in heaven, and whatever you loose on earth will be loosed in heaven"* (Matthew 16:19). He gives us authority to do all that in prayer. *We can stop things and release things!* Can you think of anything you want to stop? Or release?

Submission to the King gives us access to the kingdom. The problem with us is that sometimes we want kingdom blessings, but we don't want to be restricted by kingdom rules. We even want answers to our prayers without doing much praying. But we cannot forget that God has rescued us and will raise us up to "sit together in the heavenly places in Christ Jesus" (Ephesians 2:6). I say we owe Him big time! The least we can do is pray as He has asked us to.

You Have Authority Because the Holy Spirit Is in You

Jesus promised to send the Holy Spirit to those who believe in Him, but first He had to be crucified and resurrected. He had to triumph over death and hell and be revealed as the perfect Savior. Before all that happened, Jesus said to His disciples, "It is to your advantage that I go away; for *if I do not go away, the Helper will not come to you*; but if I depart, I will send Him to you" (John 16:7). He again referred to His Holy Spirit as the Helper when He said, "The Helper, the Holy Spirit, whom the Father will send in My name, He will teach you all things, and bring to your remembrance all things that I said to you" (John 14:26).

The Holy Spirit in us is the proof of our authority in prayer.

God could not send the Holy Spirit before that time because He cannot dwell in an unsanctified vessel. We are sanctified when we receive Jesus as our Savior, because then God sees the righteousness of Jesus in us. Then He gives us the gift of His Holy Spirit to dwell within us. I am not talking about other outpourings of the Holy Spirit. I am telling you what happens when you receive Jesus. Paul said, "No one can say that Jesus is Lord except by the Holy Spirit" (1 Corinthians 12:3).

The Holy Spirit in us is the proof that we are God's. By Him God *establishes* us, *anoints* us, and *seals* us. "He who *establishes us* with you in Christ and has *anointed us* is God, who also has *sealed us* and *given us the Spirit in our hearts as a guarantee*" (2 Corinthians 1:21-22). What an amazing gift.

The word "guarantee" is often used in the context of a business term that means money given in advance as a deposit before the rest is paid in full. The Holy Spirit in us is the deposit of Himself in advance of the fulfillment of our future with Him both in this life and the life to come in eternity. And not only that. The Holy Spirit *in* us gives us the ability to be who God wants us to be and do what He wants us to do.

Before He was crucified, Jesus said to His disciples that the Holy Spirit is "the Spirit of truth, whom the world cannot receive, because it neither sees Him nor knows Him; but you know Him, for He dwells with you and *will be in you*" (John 14:17). Because He is in us, He helps us to pray. The Holy Spirit "also helps in our weaknesses. For we do not know what we should pray for as we ought, but the Spirit Himself makes intercession for us with groanings which cannot be uttered" (Romans 8:26). You are never praying all by yourself because you have the Holy Spirit to assist you. You are never without help as to *how* to pray because He will help you when you ask Him to.

All this means you have everything you need to be a powerful prayer warrior.

You Have Authority Because You Are Called

When a soldier is called up for duty, he is given a specific assignment. He has authority to do what is necessary in order to carry out that assignment. When you are called to pray, you have full authority to carry out that assignment from God. The problem is that many are called but *not* many are listening. You *are* listening.

You must get over any doubts you have about yourself as a prayer warrior. You have the heart. You have the God-given authority. You have the desire to please God. And you have something else as well. You have the call of God on your life.

You are called to many things, and being a prayer warrior is one of them.

Being a prayer warrior is about *intercession*. Now, don't let that word become as dry to you as it sounds. It may seem like a boring word, but it is about something very exciting. I have a good analogy that I wrote about in another book on the subject of praying with other people, but it so clearly illustrates what intercession is that it's worth repeating briefly here.

In the game of football, the quarterback throws the ball to the wide receiver down the field, who is in a position to catch it and run toward his team's goal line for a touchdown. It looks as if nothing can stop him—that is, until someone from the opposing team leaps in front of the wide receiver and catches the ball instead. He *intercepts* the ball and runs it in the *opposite direction* to *his* team's goal line and makes the touchdown score for *his* team's side.

That is exactly what intercessory prayer does. And that's what you are doing as a prayer warrior. You see a situation that is headed in a wrong direction and you leap in to intercept that situation in prayer and take it the opposite direction for a victory on God's side—the team *you* are on.

There are many things God wants to do on earth and in people's lives, but if someone doesn't leap in and answer the call to pray, it won't happen.

What God saw in Israel before Jesus' time was that deception, injustice, and oppression were rampant. He was displeased because there was no one who would pray, and He *"wondered that there was no intercessor"* (Isaiah 59:16).

Later, God again sees Israel's wickedness, where even the prophets, priests, and religious leaders were oppressing, robbing, and mistreating the poor and needy. God said, "I sought for a man among them who would *make a wall*, and *stand in the gap* before Me on behalf of the land, that I should not destroy it; *but I found no one"* (Ezekiel 22:30).

To "make a wall" means to repair a break in the protective barrier the enemy had broken down. The gap is the separation between God and man that an intercessor bridges. God wanted someone to stand in that gap before Him on behalf of Israel and pray for the breach to be repaired. There was no one who would step in and intercept that situation in prayer, so God was forced to bring judgment on the nation.

I weep every time I read that passage. How terribly sad that no one heard God's call to pray and so disaster came upon the land. (Remember what I said in the first chapter about the women praying over the fault lines?) And each time I remember this passage, I pray, "Dear Lord, please don't let that be us. Help us to hear Your call to pray." How it must grieve God when He wants to do so much through us, and we are too preoccupied or distracted to hear His call to intercede. How many disasters *have* come and *will* come upon us because we are not praying?

Praying for someone, or certain people, or in this case an entire nation, means we are standing before God on their behalf. That is intercession. When God says, "Stand in the gap before Me on behalf of certain people," how can we say no? The enemy wants to break down the protective walls in every part of our lives and in the lives of others, but we can restore any breach the enemy has caused when we intercept that situation in prayer.

Every prayer warrior is an intercessor.

The crucial work of an intercessor is that we stand before God on behalf of someone else or some situation that affects others as well as ourselves and our family members. *When we pray, we are able to connect the needs of others to the outpouring of God's mercy.* God is calling you and me—the prayer warriors—to stand in the gap where the enemy has tried to destroy our marriages, families, lives, health, churches, government, finances, hopes, and purpose.

To be a prayer warrior is a high calling; the calling itself confirms your authority to do it.

Paul prayed for the Ephesians that God would give them "the spirit of wisdom and revelation in the knowledge of Him" (Ephesians 1:17). He wanted the eyes of their understanding to be enlightened so that they might know what is *"the hope of His calling...the glory of His inheritance"* and *"what is the exceeding greatness of His power toward us who believe"* (Ephesians 1:18-19). Our calling to be God's intercessor is part of our inheritance.

In order to receive an inheritance, there must be a will. In order for a will to be executed, the person who made the will has to die. "Where there is a testament, there must also of necessity be the death of the testator. For a testament is in force after men are dead, since it has no power at all while the testator lives" (Hebrews 9:16-17). But Jesus has already died for us, so the terms of His will are being fulfilled now.

We who have received Jesus are considered the called. We are not called because *we* are great. We are called because *He* is great. God does not call worldly wise and powerful people (1 Corinthians 1:26). "God has chosen the weak things of the world to put to shame the things which are mighty" (1 Corinthians 1:27). God has chosen "the things which are not, to bring to nothing the things that are" (1 Corinthians 1:28).

Do you see what that means? It means we can tell Him all the reasons we aren't enough, and He says, "That's exactly why I chose you." The reason is He wants that "no flesh should glory in His presence" (1 Corinthians 1:29). In other words, we can't take credit for something God does. So if you feel weak and you see all the reasons you don't think you can be a powerful prayer warrior, then be glad because you will have to depend on the power of God working through you. And that is exactly where God wants you—unable to be prideful or think you have done it. Rather, He wants us all fully convinced that we can do nothing without Him.

Why does God want all the glory? It's not that He is an egomaniac. It's because He is God and we are not. And He wants us to be absolutely clear about that. We've seen from previous examples how pride will cause us to stumble and fall farther than anything else can.

Your gifts and calling are no small matter to God. "The gifts and the calling of God *are* irrevocable" (Romans 11:29). That means God doesn't rescind on those. But we *can* lose our special anointing from God in our use of them when we are disobedient without a repentant heart. Don't ever minimize, devalue, or take for granted the anointing of the Lord upon you, the gifts He has given you, or His calling on your life. Always keep in your mind that "He who calls you is faithful, who also will do it" (1 Thessalonians 5:24). That means He will enable you to be the powerful prayer warrior He is calling you to be.

You Have Authority Because You Are Forgiven

Being forgiven is no small thing. Being washed clean and redeemed through Jesus' blood that was shed on the cross for you means you are forgiven of all your past sins *before* you received Him. And now you can *repent and confess* any subsequent sins before God and find forgiveness (Ephesians 1:7). That means the enemy has nothing in you unless you allow him to by believing his condemning lies instead of God's Word. Jesus has broken the enemy's ability to keep you in captivity because you are no longer separated from God (Ephesians 4:8-10).

You are a new person, so the enemy cannot throw your past up in your face. He can't say, "Look what you've done. You have no authority over me." The enemy loves to bring you down with condemnation and thereby render you powerless. But "*if anyone is in Christ, he is a new creation*; old things have passed away; behold, all things have become new" (2 Corinthians 5:17).

Don't let the enemy tell you that you have no right to pray and expect God to answer because you are imperfect or you've failed.

Those words are not God giving you revelation for your life. They are the words from the enemy of your soul wanting to discourage, demean, and destroy you. If you have unconfessed sin in your life, then confess it with a repentant heart before God. Other than that, whenever the enemy tries to discourage you from praying, deliberately thank God that your authority in prayer does not depend on your being perfect. It is because of what Jesus perfectly accomplished on the cross and *He* is perfect. When the enemy tries to bring you down, bring *him* down instead with declarations of worship to the Lord.

We can be certain every day that the war has already been won by what Jesus did on the cross. He secured our victory in His triumph over death and hell. But the war still has to be fought. It is going on now. Every battle is important. But Jesus promised, "I am with you always, even to the end of the age" (Matthew 28:20). He said, "I will never leave you nor forsake you" (Hebrews 13:5). After He was resurrected, Jesus said that all authority had been given to Him in heaven and earth (Matthew 28:18). And He delegates authority to us to pray in His name.

The scheme of the enemy is to get you to doubt that authority and everything God says about you. But remember that Jesus was raised from the dead, reigns in power over death and hell, and He pours Himself into us who believe in Him. He is the source of our strength as we are armed for spiritual warfare. He reveals our purpose to us and enables us to move into it. He empowers us. And He never *runs out* or *runs dry* because He is a deep well from which we can continuously draw living water. *God is able to do more than we can even think to ask Him for* because of the power of His Spirit working *in* us.

When you understand your authority in prayer, you will go from simply having *a prayer life* to enjoying a dynamic and exciting *life of prayer*. And that is always a good thing.

PRAYER FOR THE
PRAYER WARRIOR

THANK You, Jesus, that because I have received You I am a child of God. Thank You that You have paid the price for me to be cleansed from all sin. Thank You that You sit at the right hand of our father God and intercede for me because I believe in You and have received Your Spirit into my heart. Thank You that I am now an heir with You of all that our heavenly Father has for His children. Thank You for giving me authority to pray in Your name and to know that You hear and will answer my prayers according to Your will and Your time.

I pray that You, my Source of hope, will comfort my heart and establish me in Your Word and the work You have called me to (2 Thessalonians 2:16-17). Help me to resist all of the attempts of the enemy to discount the authority You have given me in prayer because of Your victory over death and hell on the cross. Help me to always remember the power of praying in Your name, the gift of Your Holy Spirit in me, the calling You have on my life, and the fact that You have forgiven me of all sin so the enemy can find nothing in me.

Lord, help me to be the most effective prayer warrior possible. Teach me to understand the authority You have given me in prayer. Enable me to use that authority to break down strongholds the enemy would attempt to erect in my life and in the lives of others whom You put on my heart. Keep me from doubt that I am qualified to do this because only *You* supply me with everything I need in order to pray in power.

I take my orders from You and no other. I have authority because I have You.

Enable me, Holy Spirit, to always hear Your call to pray. Teach me to rest fully on the authority You have given me as Your prayer warrior.

In Jesus' name I pray.

Beware lest anyone cheat you
through philosophy and empty deceit,
according to the tradition of men,
according to the basic principles of the world,
and not according to Christ.
For in Him dwells all the fullness
of the Godhead bodily;
and you are complete in Him,
who is the head of all principality and power.

COLOSSIANS 2:8-10

5

CONDITION YOURSELF TO BE ALL YOU CAN BE

Every good soldier knows that he or she has to stay in the best condition physically, mentally, and emotionally.

I have the greatest respect and admiration for all of our military men and women and how hard they train and work. Their bravery amazes me. They endure dangerous and difficult situations, and some face battles every day in order to protect their country and liberate oppressed people. They are deployed far away and live through long separations from their loved ones. I am beyond grateful to them all for their sacrifices. Not at any time in my life could I begin to do what they do. If it had been up to me, the United States would have surrendered to Hawaii years ago.

I have long been impressed by how hard and long Navy SEALs train and condition themselves. Their expertise is astounding. (I in no way want to imply that other branches of the military aren't doing that as well. It's just that this is the one I have read enough about to know some of what they do.) First of all, a man doesn't just wake up one day, decide to be a Navy SEAL, and then he *is* one. He has to prove himself capable, fit, excellent, and exceptional. He has to train, practice, and work excruciatingly hard to become extremely strong, sharp, skilled, knowledgeable, experienced, and prepared.

Navy SEALs take their conditioning to the extreme in order

to accomplish what seems humanly impossible. The courageous things they do are beyond most people's imagination. Their training is brutal and their skill level is the highest. How hard they are on their bodies is way beyond what any of us who are not in the military could ever begin to tolerate. They not only train their bodies, they train their minds and emotions. When they have an assignment, they plan for every possible contingency. They cannot afford to make a mistake when they are on a mission. They work together as a team—always covering each other's backs and lives—and they trust each other completely.

God wants us to prepare ourselves for spiritual warfare just as diligently as these dedicated and brave soldiers do. He wants us to be in top form. But our training is not painful. It is not near as difficult. And it brings us great rewards.

Below are the most important things we all need to do in order to stay in good condition. You don't have to do all of these perfectly *before* you become a good prayer warrior. You become a prayer warrior the moment you begin to pray with a sense of purpose. But your prayers will be more powerful and unhindered when you are in top condition—physically, mentally, emotionally, *and spiritually.*

Spend Time with God in Prayer

Part of becoming all God wants us to be is spending time with the Lord in prayer—just to be with Him and renewed by His presence. Jesus' communication with His Father God was constant. That is where He received His power. It is the same power He has for us when we come to our Father God in His name. We are empowered the same way Jesus was—by the Holy Spirit through prayer.

Our relationship with our Father God must be one of love—longing to be with Him—the same way it was with Jesus and His heavenly Father. Jesus didn't just ask for things. He wanted to walk and talk with God and be in His presence. Just as we enjoy the presence of someone we love, we enjoy being in the presence of God because we love Him and we sense His love for us. I doubt if Jesus had to *make* Himself get up and pray. He was drawn there by mutual love.

I am drawn to pray to my heavenly Father in Jesus' name because I cannot live without sensing His presence in my life. There is a need in each of our souls that cannot be filled with anything other than God. He gives us His Spirit when we receive Jesus, but He expects us to go to Him for a fresh infilling each day. It is not that the Holy Spirit becomes weak in us; it's that we get weak without His frequent refreshing. He doesn't leave or forsake us. We leave or forsake *Him*. It is we who must be renewed in Him each day. The way we meet the needs we have spiritually—and we all have them, whether we recognize or acknowledge them or not—is to spend time with our heavenly Father in prayer.

We all have human feelings, emotions, and thoughts. If we don't spend time with the Lord, we become dominated by them. But when we spend time with God, our unforgiveness, doubt, lust, hate, anxiety, and sadness becomes forgiveness, faith, purity, love, peace, and joy. When we delight ourselves in the Lord, He gives us the desires of our heart. When we *commit our ways to the Lord* and trust in Him, He brings our desires to pass as we pray about them (Psalm 37:4-5).

Live in a Way That Pleases God

In order to live in a way that pleases God, you have to make it a lifelong goal to understand exactly what pleases Him. We can't rely on guesswork, hearsay, or old wives' tales. (We don't even know who these old wives are.)

The first way to please God is to keep His commandments and laws. That's why the biggest part of preparing yourself to be all God created you to be is to become more and more solid in His Word. That means reading something in the Bible every day. That's because if we don't, we become lax. We lose it. When the Word becomes distant in us, we grow distant from God.

Paul said, "We must give the more earnest heed to the things we have heard, lest we drift away" (Hebrews 2:1). We cannot allow our heart to drift away from the things of God because it surely will. We're like that. Our nature is selfish. We drift toward self-focus unless we focus on God every day. The heart of a prayer warrior is strong, solid, and full of faith. The Word of God infused into it each day makes it that way.

The Word of God is living. When we live in it and let it live in us, it gives us more life. Because the Bible is inspired by the Holy Spirit, as you read it the Holy Spirit brings it alive to your mind and soul. Every time you read it He will breathe greater understanding into your spirit. This doesn't happen unless a person has been spiritually reborn. That's because the Holy Spirit gives us spiritual understanding we did not have before our spiritual eyes were opened.

The Word of God is powerful and "sharper than any two-edged sword, piercing even to the division of soul and spirit, and of joints and marrow, and is a discerner of the thoughts and intents of the heart" (Hebrews 4:12). It reveals discrepancies between your soul and spirit, in case your spirit wants to obey God and your soul doesn't. But we must not just *read* the Word; we must *live* it. Paul said, "Not the *hearers* of the law are just in the sight of God, but the *doers* of the law will be justified" (Romans 2:13).

Another thing that pleases God is your love for Him. Jesus equated keeping the Commandments and laws with loving Him. He said, "If anyone loves Me, he will keep My word; and My Father will love him, and We will come to him and make Our home with him" (John 14:23). The promise here is that if we love God, we will obey Him, and we will then have His presence. Who doesn't want the presence of God dwelling *with* them? When we love God and keep His commandments, we truly live *in Him* and He *in us.*

Don't get confused by the idea that God is everywhere. That is true. But the *fullness of His presence* is only where He is invited to be and only where there is a pure vessel in which He can dwell.

He will not dwell in the stench of sin and unrepentant disobedience. When Paul said, "I die daily," he was talking about dying to
sin (1 Corinthians 15:31). Sin will always be our master if we don't
confess and repent of it immediately when we realize we have done
something that is not pleasing to God. The consequences for sin are
so deathly that we lose all power when we succumb to it.

Our conscience will always tell us the truth. We can't hide anything from God because He knows and sees everything. "There is no
creature hidden from His sight, but all things are naked and open
to the eyes of Him to whom we must give account" (Hebrews 4:13).
As a prayer warrior, God uses us powerfully to affect situations and
people—not only in *our* lives and the lives of our family members,
friends, community, and country, but all over the world as well—
and we cannot let our own sin deter us.

One of the reasons Jesus came was to destroy the works of the
enemy. "He who sins is of the devil, for the devil has sinned from
the beginning. *For this purpose the Son of God was manifested, that
He might destroy the works of the devil.* Whoever has been born of
God does not sin, for His seed remains in him; and he cannot sin,
because he has been born of God" (1 John 3:8-9). Don't even think
about being a prayer warrior until you have repented of any sin in
your life because the enemy will use it against you. Take care of that
right away. *You cannot oppose the devil's plans in prayer if you align
yourself with him in your personal life.*

We are not the type of people who will murder someone or rob
a bank. We have a heart for the Lord and want to obey His commandments. But we might give in to doubt. And doubt is a sin. Or
we might say or do something that shows a lack of love on our part.
That does not please God at all. We know the things we do that do
not glorify God. Our conscience tells us and so does God's Word.

When we love God, we keep His commandments and do what
pleases Him. As a result our conscience is clear. "If our heart does
not condemn us, we have confidence toward God. And *whatever*

we ask we receive from Him, because we keep His commandments and do those things that are pleasing in His sight" (1 John 3:21-22). This is crucial to our receiving answers to our prayers.

Think back to any time when you have allowed sin in your heart—even the sin of doubt or lovelessness. Can you see the ways in which it brought death in your body, in your relationships, in your work, in your life? Paul asks, "What fruit did you have then in the things of which you are now ashamed? For the end of those things is death" (Romans 6:21). Renounce sin as your master. Say, "I am not a slave of sin. I am a slave of righteousness because Jesus has set me free from sin." You are not talking to the devil. You are declaring the truth, and that is part of taking dominion over the powers of evil.

We all have the ability to sin. Anyone who doesn't think so is destined to fall. "All have sinned and fall short of the glory of God" (Romans 3:23). But we *choose* whether to keep on in that way or not. We have a choice to refuse our sin nature and partake of the divine nature. God has given to you "exceedingly great and precious promises, that through these you may be partakers of the divine nature, having escaped the corruption that is in the world through lust" (2 Peter 1:4). Our lust is that we want what we want when we want it. But we can choose to want what *God* wants.

When people ignore the truth and establish false views of God and the Bible in order to justify themselves, they then do what they *want*. You can see this in every false religion built on another man other than Jesus. There is always sin inherent in their teaching. When they reject God and His law, He gives them over to their own self-destructive lifestyles. But God has given us a way to become more like Him and escape all that. When we receive Jesus we become "dead indeed to sin, but alive to God in Christ Jesus our Lord" (Romans 6:11). We no longer have to allow such error into our lives, because we can choose to not give place to it (Romans 6:12).

When we walk with Jesus, we don't live apart from Him and His ways. Sin becomes unnatural to us. If it doesn't, then we don't really know the Lord. "Whoever sins has neither seen Him nor known Him" (1 John 3:6). That doesn't mean we never sin, because we all do, but it is not our way of life. We are not characterized by a spirit of rebellion or lawlessness. We are not powerless against the things that pollute our lives.

A prayer warrior must be separate from sin. If you have sin in your life, it will weaken you. The enemy knows it and will use it to harm you. Sin will always separate you from God, and you won't see your prayers answered until you turn away from sin and back to God. Paul says that once we get free of these things we are to "stand fast therefore in the liberty by which Christ has made us free, and do not be entangled again with a yoke of bondage" (Galatians 5:1). That means don't go back to a life of anything that is below the standard Jesus set for you. You are better than that. It makes Jesus' death on the cross seem pointless.

Freedom in Christ is not a license to do whatever we want. Though we are free from the control of sin or evil, we must never believe that we are so spiritual we cannot fail. We can. But if we always follow the leading of the Holy Spirit, He will enable us to live the life God has for us. And *that* always pleases God.

Acknowledge God's Call to Holiness

One of the many things God calls us to is to be holy as He is. Now, before you put the book down and say, "There is no way I can do that," I want to agree with you. There is no way any one of us can be holy on our own. It is only by the power of the Holy Spirit working in us that we are enabled to be holy. Paul said, "God did not call us to uncleanness, but in holiness" (1 Thessalonians 4:7). He went on to say that if we reject this, we are rejecting God, "who has also given us His Holy Spirit" (1 Thessalonians 4:8). In other words we are rejecting everything we need to be holy.

Holiness is a desire of the heart to please God and an invitation to the Holy Spirit to do what it takes in us to make us more like Him.

The promise that God will dwell among us and be our Father should be enough to draw us toward living a life that is devoted to pleasing Him, cleansing "ourselves from all filthiness of the flesh and spirit, perfecting holiness in the fear of God" (2 Corinthians 7:1). When we fully recognize all Jesus has done for us, we will do what it takes to live a holy life that is pleasing to Him. "Everyone who has this hope in Him purifies himself, just as He is pure" (1 John 3:3). Being a slave of God leads us to a life of holiness (Romans 6:22). And a life of holiness is for our greatest good. All of God's ways and laws are for our benefit. When we are in pursuit of holiness, we are in a place of great safety and blessing.

A life of holiness is a life of power and significance because God can use you powerfully and significantly.

We can't always recognize our own sin apart from reading God's Word. But while the Word enlightens our conscience about sin, it cannot *make* us holy. Only Jesus saves us from sin, and only the Holy Spirit dwelling in us makes it possible for us to live a holy life. In order to live a holy life, you must be dedicated wholly to God.

Get Rid of Anything in Your Life That Is Not Glorifying to God

God wants you to separate yourself from anything that separates you from Him. That includes any bad habits, stubbornness, inflexibility, bondage, bad influences, unhealthy practices, or possessions that are not glorifying to Him. These things can be in our lives and we don't even recognize them.

None of us is perfect. We are all capable of getting involved in things that displease God, even the best among us. But the more we walk with the Lord, the more we become aware of what grieves Him. And the better we know God, the more we do not want to grieve Him.

God rejects anyone who dishonors Him.

Separating ourselves from things that do not glorify God is a matter of reverencing Him. It means we have the fear of God in our heart. And having the fear of God means we know there are consequences for *not* having it—the greatest of which is separation from God. No one who has felt the love, peace, and transforming presence of God wants to ever experience any distance from Him.

Corruption enters in the hearts of people who have no fear of God.

When people feel they don't have to answer to God for what they do or possess, they are courting a rebellious spirit. If you see a Christian violating the will of God blatantly and arrogantly, you can be sure that person has shut out the voice of the Holy Spirit to his heart a long time ago.

We cannot hang on to anything that does not please God without being convicted of it by the Holy Spirit. But if we continue to hang on to these things even after we are made aware of them, we are flirting with the enemy's camp. We must ask God to show us anything from which we need to separate ourselves. Sometimes we don't realize what we have allowed into our lives until we ask God and the Holy Spirit reveals it.

Get rid of any bad attitude, destructive habit, wrong mind-set, unhealthy practice, or forbidden activity that hinders your spiritual growth and development. This is not to be legalistic. It is to be aware of the leading of the Holy Spirit as you seek His guidance. Say, "Lord, show me if there is anything in my life that should not be there, or anything that displeases You and hurts me physically, mentally, or spiritually." When He shows you something, ask Him to help you rid your life of everything that is not of Him.

Refuse All Pride

Pride is the main characteristic of the enemy. When we fall into pride, we align ourselves with the enemy's plans. Because we are all made in the image of God, we must never think of ourselves as worth *less* than God sees us. Nor should we think of ourselves as worth *more* than anyone else. No one is to "think of himself more highly than he ought to think, but to think soberly" (Romans 12:3). Pride causes us to compare ourselves to other people when we should only compare ourselves to God's standards. "If anyone thinks himself to be something, when he is nothing, he deceives himself" (Galatians 6:3).

Pride is dangerous and we must not give in to it because "God resists the proud, but gives grace to the humble" (James 4:6).

God wants us to "walk worthy of our calling"—whatever we are called to personally—but He does not want us to allow even one second of pride regarding it (Ephesians 4:1). We are not to abuse ourselves with self-criticism and lament what we think we lack, either. This also is a form of pride. The truth is that we are not worth more because of what we do but because of what Jesus has done.

Ask God to reveal any pride in you. When you see it, resist it by confessing it to God and ask Him to help you get free of it.

Fulfill God's Command to Love Others

It should be easy to distinguish between the children of God and the spawn of the enemy, but sometimes it is not. Jesus said this difference is most clearly seen in whether a person loves his brothers and sisters in Christ. One of the things the Holy Spirit does in us is give us a love for others we didn't have before we knew the Lord. John said, "In this the children of God and the children of the devil are manifest: whoever does not practice righteousness is not of God, *nor is he who does not love his brother*" (1 John 3:10).

When we don't have love in our heart for others, we are living a dead life. "He who does not love his brother abides in death. Whoever hates his brother is a murderer, and you know that no murderer has eternal life abiding in him" (1 John 3:14-15).

Yikes! It can't get any clearer. We are the same as a murderer when we don't love others. And that does not predict a good future of blessing from God.

To the extent it is up to you, try to live in harmony with your spiritual family. I am not saying you have to be best friends with everybody in the body of Christ, but to the best of your ability be at peace with them. Some people look for reasons to be loveless to others more than they look for ways to show the love of God. You must be different. Especially because you are a prayer warrior for Him. You are in the service. *His* service. Serving *Him*. You must represent Him well.

While you can't make someone be different than whom they choose to be, you can *pray* for them. And that's what prayer warriors do. When people are loveless toward you, pray for God to convict their heart about it. You are a prayer warrior because you have love in your heart toward God. When you pray for others, you do it because you love Him. And as you are praying, *He* gives you His love for that person or those people.

Ask God to give you more love for others than you have ever had before.

Don't Be Careless with Your Body

God is very serious about this. He wants us to love and appreciate our own body and do nothing to harm or destroy it. You must never be careless, abusive, or neglectful in the treatment of your body because it is a gift from God, and His Holy Spirit dwells in you as a precious gift as well. You are never entitled to do whatever you want. "Do you not know that you are the temple of God and *that* the Spirit of God dwells in you? If anyone defiles the temple of God, God will destroy him. For the temple of God is holy, which *temple* you are" (1 Corinthians 3:16-17).

God doesn't like us abusing our bodies. And He makes that clear when He says if we defile our body in any way, He will give us over to the destruction we seem to be courting.

That sounds very serious to me.

Mistreatment of our body with flagrant disregard for the

consequences of what we are doing to it does not please God. If you already know what you are doing wrong, ask God to help you make the right choices. If you are not sure, ask Him to show you what you should do differently. The Holy Spirit will help you do the right thing in every situation. But you have to want His help.

Separate Yourself from the Ungodly

Sin contaminates. And it doesn't even have to be *your* sin. Just as leaven ferments through the entire loaf of bread waiting to be baked, the influence of sinful people you associate with spreads to you. Even when you are trying to help someone out of their misguided life, if they continue to resist your efforts, you must separate yourself from them and release them into God's hands. Paul said, "Do not be deceived: Evil company corrupts good habits" (1 Corinthians 15:33). And don't think you can impose your morality on others who are unbelievers because that doesn't work.

Be careful not to spend time with unbelievers who are into idolatrous practices and thereby yoke yourself in relationships that compromise your walk with God. "Do not be unequally yoked together with unbelievers. For what fellowship has righteousness with lawlessness? And what communion has light with darkness?" (2 Corinthians 6:14). "*Come out from among them and be separate*, says the Lord. Do not touch what is unclean, and I will receive you" (2 Corinthians 6:17). Separate yourself from them.

The more we are careful about our walk with the Lord and want to please God, the more we live in the purity He has called us to. This will allow us to become more effective as prayer warriors and in life. Paul said, "Have no fellowship with the unfruitful works of darkness, but rather expose them" (Ephesians 5:11). We don't have to be unloving or rude to people. We don't have to be legalistic and cold, thereby turning people off to the vibrant life in the Lord that awaits them. More people are pushed away from receiving Jesus by the unloving and harsh ways of Christians who are better at criticism and judgment than they are at showing the love of God. Ask God to show you if you have left yourself open for an enemy attack because you have allowed someone into your life in a way that allows them to affect you more than you affect them for God's kingdom.

Don't Dwell on What You Are Not

Too many believers don't know what God says about them. They think about what *someone else* has said about them, or what they keep *telling themselves* in all their self-criticism. Don't let this happen to you because this is not of the Lord and it only weakens you.

Don't allow the enemy to put thoughts in your head of all that you *aren't*. Instead, think about what you *can* be. Don't dwell on what you think you *should be*. Think about what God says you *are*.

I left this section with few words because it cannot be said any clearer than the paragraph above. My pastor, Pastor James, said that and it really stuck in my mind. I could write a thousand more words, but it will still come down to that. Read the paragraph above a few more times. Write it down and put it on your mirror, your nightstand, or your refrigerator door. This is very important. You cannot become all God made you to be if you doubt what He says about you.

Don't let the enemy tell you that you aren't good enough, right enough, holy enough, loveable enough, or just not enough. I say, "Enough!" Don't allow the enemy to have the satisfaction of convincing you that you can never become all God made you to be. It's not true. Focus on pleasing God and finding out what He has called you to do. Recognize it. Pray about it. Get involved in it.

Walk in a Way to Produce the Fruit of the Spirit

When we completely surrender our lives to the Lord and are led by His Spirit, He will produce the fruit of His Spirit in us. "The fruit of the Spirit is love, joy, peace, longsuffering, kindness, goodness, faithfulness, gentleness, self-control. Against such there is no law" (Galatians 5:22-23). We all need these nine character traits to be forming in us at all times.

Even though our righteousness comes from what Jesus did on the cross, that doesn't give us the *right* to function in the power of the Holy Spirit without living moral lives of integrity. Doing God's work is not for the disobedient or unholy. "Those who are Christ's have crucified the flesh with its passions and desires. If we live in the Spirit, let us also walk in the Spirit" (Galatians 5:24-25). When you are pure in heart, that keeps the lines of communication open between you and God. And it opens up the channel through which His Holy Spirit can lead you. And that is the key—being led by the Holy Spirit.

When you choose to be led by the Spirit, you are *choosing* to walk in the light. "You were once darkness, but now you are light in the Lord. Walk as children of light *(for the fruit of the Spirit is in all goodness, righteousness, and truth)*, finding out what is acceptable to the Lord" (Ephesians 5:8-10). And because evil is proliferating, we must "walk circumspectly, not as fools but as wise, redeeming the time, because the days are evil. Therefore *do not be unwise, but understand what the will of the Lord is*" (Ephesians 5:15-17).

We cannot afford to live outside the will of God.

Ask God to help you understand His will and enable you to always walk being led by His Spirit, and you will continuously produce the fruit of His Spirit in your life.

Be Renewed in Your Mind

The world system is godless. Godless people do not seek God. Their god is their appetite, lust, desire, ambition, pride, and power. They want control, and they will do whatever it takes to get it—even lie, cheat, destroy, and kill. (Sound familiar?) Their god is the enemy of God and the enemy of all believers.

Whoever conforms to the world's system is joining the enemy of God. I am not talking about the beautiful physical world that God created and all of His goodness in it. I am talking about the spirit in the world that is anti-God and anti-Christ and is controlled by the anti-Christ spirit. We must not align ourselves with it. The enemy blinds the minds of people to this spirit, but it is still their choice to not believe God. "Even if our gospel is veiled, it is veiled to those who are perishing, *whose minds the god of this age has blinded*, who do not believe, lest the light of the gospel of the glory of Christ, who is the image of God, should shine on them" (2 Corinthians 4:3-4). Those whose minds are blinded will never see the beauty of the Lord.

God wants us to resist the anti-Christ way of thinking. The Bible says, "You should no longer walk as the rest of the Gentiles walk, *in the futility of their mind, having their understanding darkened*, being alienated from the life of God, because of the ignorance that is in them, *because of the blindness of their heart*; who, being past feeling, have given themselves over to lewdness, to work all uncleanness with greediness" (Ephesians 4:17-19).

The Bible says, "Do not love the world or the things in the world. If anyone loves the world, the love of the Father is not in him. For all that is in the world—the lust of the flesh, the lust of the eyes, and the pride of life—is not of the Father but is of the world. And *the world is passing away, and the lust of it; but he who does the will of God abides forever*" (1 John 2:15-17).

God tells us to "put off, concerning your former conduct, the old man which grows corrupt according to the deceitful lusts, and be *renewed in the spirit of your mind*, and that you put on the new man which was created according to God, in true righteousness and holiness" (Ephesians 4:23-24). The way we resist that world spirit is to have our mind renewed and have clarity in our thoughts. Thank God every day that He gives us the mind of Christ.

Be Forgiving at All Times

Being unforgiving toward someone takes way too much time and energy and is far beneath who God has made you to be. Don't waste your life on it. Yes, people can hurt us so badly that we want to take revenge by never letting go in our mind of what they have done. But way too much is made of forgiving others in the Bible—by Jesus, especially—to ignore this command of God. We do so at our own peril. Jesus said, "If you forgive men their trespasses, your heavenly Father will also forgive you. *But if you do not forgive men their trespasses, neither will your Father forgive your trespasses*" (Matthew 6:14-15). It doesn't get any clearer than that.

God won't even hear our prayers unless we get rid of unforgiveness. "If I regard iniquity in my heart, the Lord will not hear" (Psalm 66:18). It's not that the Lord *cannot* hear our prayer, but He *chooses not to*. Sometimes we think we have already dealt with a person or an issue, yet it comes creeping back into our hearts. That's because there can be layers of unforgiveness, especially if the offense was severe or happened over a long period of time.

If you have trouble forgiving someone, ask God to help you. He will. When you forgive others, you are made free from the torture that comes with *not* forgiving. Torture that the enemy will use against you to weaken and destroy you.

You don't want to hinder your prayers from being answered and stop up your life from receiving the blessings God has for you. You don't want to be weakened in your spiritual battle. You want to be empowered by the all-powerful God you serve. Ask God to reveal any unforgiveness in you so that you can be rid of it.

Jesus gives us complete forgiveness for our sins, so we must lay down all guilt and receive it. Not being convinced that you are completely forgiven of your sins means you have to carry around heavy baggage of condemnation. That's just as bad as unforgiveness, which is a heavy burden your shoulders were not built to carry. It doesn't allow you the freedom to be the person you are called to be. Because He has forgiven you, you must forgive others.

Watch What You Say

What we say can compromise our walk with God. That's why we must ask the Holy Spirit to monitor what we speak *before* we speak it. The good news is that God can change our heart to affect the overflow of our words. "He who would love life and see good days, let him refrain his tongue from evil, and his lips from speaking deceit. Let him turn away from evil and do good; let him seek peace and pursue it. For the eyes of the LORD are on the righteous, and His ears are open to their prayers; but the face of the LORD is against those who do evil" (1 Peter 3:10-12).

There is a connection between what we say—whether it is evil or not—and answered prayer. God hears our prayers when our words reflect His truth.

When we have God's Word living in us, and the Holy Spirit in us activating that power, it regenerates and renews our heart the way nothing else can. And the result is that good things flow out of our heart and are reflected in our speech. When we open to the truth of God's Word, we become spiritually alive. It renews our life every day. And it never fails.

Jesus told us to pray, "Your will be done on earth as it is in heaven" (Matthew 6:10). It must be *our* will to do our *Father's* will just as it was with Jesus. Our old self is who we were before we met Jesus. Our new self is who we are now that we have received Jesus and have been reborn in our spirit. Our old self says, "My way is best." Our new self says, "*God's* way is best." We have to put off our old self and put on the new.

When we delight ourselves in the Lord, we want what God wants. We align our heart with God's and submit our will to His will in order to be effective in prayer. That means praying that our words will always be glorifying to Him.

Even if you are a prayer warrior already, don't stop preparing yourself to be an even stronger one. God doesn't want you to stay as a child. He wants you to grow in Him so He can change you into

His image. He wants to use you in powerful ways, especially as His return draws nearer. "Do you not know that those who run in a race all run, but one receives the prize? Run in such a way that you may obtain it" (1 Corinthians 9:24). Prepare yourself every day to be all God wants you to be, so you can run the race and win the prize.

Prayer for the
Prayer Warrior

LORD, help me to always have a clear conscience before You. Let there be nothing in me that gives the enemy a reason to think he has any kind of invitation to undermine what You want to do in my life. Help me to not give in to fleshly desires. Enable me to be holy as You are holy, for I know it is only by Your Spirit working in me that this happens. Help me to keep my mind focused on serving You (1 Peter 1:15-16). I know I was redeemed with something far more precious than gold, and that is the blood of Your Son (1 Peter 1:18-19). Help me to live in a manner worthy of that.

Teach me to become the prayer warrior You have called me to be. Help me to pray without ceasing so that I can be in constant contact with You. I bring every thought, fear, concern, and longing to You. Help me to "put on tender mercies, kindness, humility, meekness, longsuffering" (Colossians 3:12). Enable me to live, "not lagging in diligence, fervent in spirit, serving the Lord, rejoicing in hope, patient in tribulation, continuing steadfastly in prayer" (Romans 12:11-12).

Lord, help me to be holy by separating myself from anything that is not holy in Your eyes. Teach me to be separate from anything that is not glorifying to You. Teach me to stand in the liberty by which You have freed me (Galatians 5:1). I don't want to live below Your high standard for my life. Show me anything from which I need to separate myself. Thank You that You will complete the work You have begun in me (Philippians 1:6).

Show me where I have pride so I can repent of it. I don't

want to fall into being prideful and fall out of Your grace (James 4:6). Show me how to resist pride in myself the way You resist those who entertain it. Enable me to love others the way You do. I know that to do otherwise does not please You (1 John 3:10). Give me Your love for others in a way that causes it to overflow my heart and pour out in my actions and prayers toward them.

Teach me how to take care of my body, for I know it is where Your Spirit dwells and doing anything to harm myself displeases You. Help me to know the right things to do and convict me when I don't do them. Enable me to always walk led by Your Spirit so that the fruit of Your Spirit is produced in me. Fill me with a fresh flow of Your love, joy, peace, patience, kindness, goodness, faithfulness, gentleness, and self-control (Galatians 5:22-23). Help me to stop thinking about what I am *not*, and instead focus on what I *can* be. Help me to not worry over what I *should* be, but focus on what *You* say I am.

In Jesus' name I pray.

Do not be conformed to this world,
but be transformed by the renewing of your mind,
that you may prove what is that
good and acceptable and perfect will of God.

ROMANS 12:2

6

Put On Your Protective Armor Each Morning

Before each specific assignment Navy SEALs are given, they thoroughly assess their equipment. Each item they have with them is chosen for a specific reason—to protect themselves, fight the enemy, win the battle, survive, and return safely. Every aspect of their equipment is of the best quality and must be in perfect working order or condition. Because all of this has to be carried with them on their body, they assemble their camouflage uniform with precision and great thought. They know they can't go into battle safely or effectively if they are missing something important or carrying extra baggage. Everything they take with them is designed to facilitate and anticipate their every need. By the time they are on a mission they are more than ready.

As prayer warriors we must do the same. God doesn't want us carrying anything that is unnecessary because it will weigh us down and hinder what He has called us to do. And we must not go to battle without the things we need in order to win. Our battle is spiritual, and what we accomplish in the spirit realm is as important as what the highly trained, prepared, and equipped soldier does in the physical. We must know our weapons and be highly skilled in using them. (More about that in the next chapter, "Become Skilled with Your Spiritual Weapons.") But first we must put on the armor God has given us in order to stand strong against the enemy.

The apostle Paul said, "Be strong in the Lord and in the power of His might. *Put on the whole armor of God, that you may be able to stand against the wiles of the devil*" (Ephesians 6:10-11). He didn't say, "If you are smart you might take up the *whole* armor." Or, "If you feel like it and have the time, take up the armor." Or, "Try to take up the armor at least once or twice a year." God's Word says, "Take up the whole armor of God" (Ephesians 6:13). This is not suggested, it is *commanded.*

The Bible would not have told us to take up the whole armor of God in order to withstand evil if evil could have been withstood without doing that.

To "stand against" literally means to stand in front of and in opposition to the forces and plans of evil. It means to be the one standing after the battle. It also means to stand in preparation for the *next* battle. Standing against the wiles of the devil certainly doesn't mean do nothing. If we are to do nothing until He comes, why do we need to wrestle against the enemy? "We do not wrestle against flesh and blood, but against principalities, against powers, against the rulers of the darkness of this age, against spiritual hosts of wickedness in the heavenly places" (Ephesians 6:12). Why does Jesus give us spiritual weapons to withstand evil forces if He doesn't want us to use them?

The reason we must put on the whole armor of God is to withstand evil. We don't war against people, but against a spiritual hierarchy of invisible power.

The forces of evil are invisible powers with a structure and specific levels of authority. We are not only to use our armor to protect and defend ourselves from them—as important as that is—but also to go on the offensive against them as well. When we do that, we close doors to the enemy and open doors to the will of God to be done on earth. We advance God's kingdom.

Every soldier knows exactly when the time is right to put on his protective battle gear. Prayer warriors need to put on the armor of

God every day because the war is always going on. New battles continually need to be fought so that evil will be driven back, the kingdom of God advanced, and the will of God be done. Our spiritual armor not only protects us from the enemy, it also gives us what we need in order to push against him.

In order to put on the armor of God, we must first identify what the armor is. Paul talked about how to identify and battle the forces of evil using the Roman soldiers as his model. They were by far the most powerful army of that time, and he relates the pieces of armor they had with what God has given us in the spirit realm. The following is what he said:

- Stand therefore, having *girded your waist with truth*
- having *put on the breastplate of righteousness*,
- and having *shod your feet with the preparation of the gospel of peace*;
- above all, *taking the shield of faith* with which you will be able to quench all the fiery darts of the wicked one.
- And take *the helmet of salvation*,
- and *the sword of the Spirit,* which is the word of God;
- *praying always with all prayer* and supplication in the Spirit,
- *being watchful* to this end with all perseverance and supplication for all the saints (Ephesians 6:14-18).

This is not hard, so don't give me that look that says, "This is sounding like too much work." Remember what I said in chapter 1 about what is *really* too much work? You can do this! We can all do this because we stand strong in *God's* power and strength, not our own. That takes the pressure off of us trying to do it ourselves. We just have to *show up and pray*.

Some people think that because Jesus accomplished everything on the cross, *we* don't have to do anything at all. But if that's true, why did Jesus teach us to pray, "Deliver us from the evil one" (Matthew 6:13)? Why did Paul say to "pray without ceasing" (1 Thessalonians 5:17)? Yes, the *victory* over evil was accomplished on the cross, *but the enemy is still here.* He is a defeated enemy, but he is still waging the war. We don't want him winning any battles on our watch, especially as long as we can be part of the force God has called to stop him. We must have the whole armor of God protecting us at all times so we can stand successfully against the enemy's plans for not only our life, but also the lives of others.

When you get up every day, put on your protective armor. Don't leave your day to chance. Take possession of it and surrender it to the Lord. Don't let it get out of control and give the enemy an invitation to have input. You need this armor to stop any onslaught of the enemy's destructive arrows into your life and the lives of those you care about—both now and in the future.

Put on the following pieces of armor God gives you.

Gird Your Waist with the Truth

Roman soldiers girded their waist with something similar to what a weight lifter wears to give him strength and support so he won't hurt the core of his body. It enabled the soldiers to stand stronger against their enemy.

We, too, need that kind of support to give us strength in our spiritual core. That means we must tightly surround ourselves with truth and not allow for anything other than the truth to enter into our thinking or situation. It means asking God to keep us undeceived so that we never allow deception to take root. Knowing the truth liberates us from all possibility of deception and illuminates any darkness in our life.

This doesn't mean just know *about* the truth. It means know it so that it becomes part of you and you live it. And it is not just *any* truth that sets you free. It is *God's* truth. Jesus said, "If you abide in My word, you are My disciples indeed. And *you shall know the truth, and the truth shall make you free*" (John 8:31-32). When we wrap God's truth around us, it protects us by strengthening our core being.

The enemy uses lies to confuse people and fill them with anxiety and fear. The apostle John said, "We know that we are of God, and the whole world lies under the sway of the wicked one" (1 John 5:19). The enemy's lies completely mess up our thinking and weaken us if we believe them. Every day we must combat his lies with God's truth.

Put On the Breastplate of Righteousness

A Roman soldier's metal breastplate covered his chest and kept him from being fatally wounded in the heart. Jesus' perfect righteousness is what covers *our* heart, and that is what God sees when He looks at us. But we still have to put on righteousness like a soldier puts on a bulletproof vest. That means we must choose to live God's way. We cannot be protected if we deliberately walk outside the ways and will of God.

Our decision every day must be to live a righteous life—not in our own strength, but by the enablement of the Holy Spirit in us. We must acknowledge that we depend on God and choose to live our life for *Him*. Even though we *are* a new creation, we still must decide to *live* like we are. When we make that choice every day to live in a righteous manner, our life is covered and our heart is protected.

How many attacks of the enemy on people's lives could have been avoided if only they had decided that morning to live God's way? With each step we take apart from God's ways, the stronghold of the enemy becomes more entrenched.

Our breastplate of righteousness is the righteousness of Jesus *in* us. It protects our heart from any mortal wounds and assures us that the enemy can never destroy us because of sin. For example, harboring anger is a sin. The Bible says, "Be angry, and do not sin: do not let the sun go down on your wrath, *nor give place to the devil*" (Ephesians 4:26-27). But we can get straight with God at any time by confessing and repenting of our sins. Don't let the enemy have any ground upon which he can accuse you. Every day say, "Lord, show me anything in me that is not right in Your eyes so I can confess it before You, because I choose to live *Your* way."

Shoe Your Feet with the Preparation of the Gospel of Peace

Every soldier learns to protect his feet. They have special shoes or boots for that purpose. Roman soldiers had strong military shoes studded on the bottom of the soles in a way similar to cleats. Properly shod feet can stand strong against the enemy and keep from slipping. As a prayer warrior, we need to have the foundation we walk in to be solid and protective. The good news is Jesus already prepared that for us. Having peace *with* God and peace *in* God is an unshakeable foundation from which we can defend ourselves and stay standing strong.

The word "preparation" means that the gospel of peace has already been accomplished. That is, it is already prepared for you. You just have to walk in it. God has peace for us that is beyond our comprehension. It is not that we can't imagine having peace; it's just that we can't imagine having that kind of peace in the midst of the things we experience here on earth.

The enemy wants to steal our peace and keep us stirred up, anxious, fearful, upset, and always in a stance of waiting for something terrible to happen at any minute. The enemy wants us unable to forget the terrible things that occurred in the past and instead remember them as though they happened yesterday. God has healing for upsetting memories. It's not that He gives us amnesia. We still remember that it happened, but not incessantly and not with the same pain and torture.

Peace is more than just having a good night's sleep—although many people would think even that to be a miracle—but it is peace in every part of your being all the time. It is a place you live because of the One who lives in you.

Jesus made it possible for us to have the peace that passes all understanding—the kind that carries us, stabilizes us, grounds us, and keeps us from slipping.

Take the Shield of Faith

Every soldier needs something to shield and protect him from the weapons of the enemy. In Roman times, the weapons were arrows and swords. The soldiers sometimes shot flaming arrows and darts over protective walls to set people and their dwelling places on fire. In the same way, the enemy shoots spiritual arrows and darts at us designed to pierce our heart with discouragement and make us fearful, anxious, uncertain, or incapacitated. The shield we have against these arrows of the enemy is our faith, and it is powerful protection from all that.

We all—even unbelievers—have faith in something or someone. We have faith that the pharmacist won't poison us when we have our prescription from the doctor filled. We have faith that we can walk into a mall and not be killed. But lately our faith seems to be waning with regard to these kinds of things. However, when we put our faith in God and His Son, we start out having small faith, but our faith *grows* stronger as we read the Word and spend time with God in prayer.

How do we know our faith is strong enough to be a protective shield from the enemy? We know because God's Word says that *it is our faith in God* and *His faithfulness to us* that becomes a shield for us. God said to Abram, "Do not be afraid, Abram, *I am your shield, your exceedingly great reward*" (Genesis 15:1). When we put our faith in God and His Word, He is our shield and defense. Now *that* is something we can have faith in.

Even if our faith is shaky one day—it happens to all of us until we learn to have faith no matter what we see happening around us—we can still depend on the faithfulness of God to cover us and increase our faith as we hide ourselves in Him. So when you feel the enemy trying to tempt you in your weakest area, increase your faith by saying, "No temptation has overtaken you except such as is common to man; but *God is faithful*, who will not allow you to be tempted beyond what you are able, but with the temptation will also make the way of escape, that you may be able to bear it" (1 Corinthians 10:13).

When the enemy comes to test your allegiance to the Lord, focus on God, His Word, and His faithfulness to do what He says. Say, "The LORD God is a sun and shield; the LORD will give grace and glory; *no good thing will he withhold from those who walk uprightly*" (Psalm 84:11).

Faith dissolves fear and makes us courageous. Jesus said to the ruler of the synagogue, "Do not be afraid; only believe" (Mark 5:36). Faith opens up unlimited possibilities. Jesus said, "*If you can believe, all things are possible to him who believes*" (Mark 9:23).

Our faith must grow strong enough to believe for the impossible because we believe in the God of the impossible, and with Him all things are possible.

Take the Helmet of Salvation

The helmet protects a soldier's head. Our spiritual helmet protects our head as well. And what does our head most need protection from? The lies of the enemy, of course. The enemy wants to keep you from understanding—and living in—all that salvation means for you. He wants you blinded to everything Jesus died for you to have. He wants you convinced that you are worthless, rejected, weak, bad, unimportant, hopeless, and unlovable. Or if he can't get you to think that way, he tempts you to go in the opposite direction and be full of pride. Either way, you fall.

Too often, wrong thoughts about ourselves usually have a root somewhere in our childhood. Certain misguided people caused us to come to the wrong conclusions about who we are, and the enemy never ceases to reinforce those ideas. He doesn't want us to find out who we really are in the Lord and what God has for us. He wants to fill our minds with feelings of guilt, helplessness, and misery. He doesn't want us to understand all that Jesus did for us on the cross because he knows when we put on that helmet of salvation and are transformed through the renewing of our mind, we will be able to see ourselves as God sees us—someone worth dying for.

God loves us, but we too often see ourselves as unloved. God sees us as chosen and accepted, but we may see ourselves as rejected. God sees us from the perspective of who He created us to be, but we too often see ourselves from our limitations instead of our possibilities. The helmet of salvation gives us new perspective of ourselves that aligns with our heavenly Father's view of us.

My husband and I wrote a song years ago called "When I Accepted You." I wrote the lyrics about receiving the Lord before I fully realized the profound consequences of doing that. (Debby Boone recorded this on two of her albums, *Choose Life*, and the most recent, *Morningstar*. Please visit www.debbyboone.com.) I have included the words here because they sum up what salvation means in the clearest and simplest way.

> You were poor
> So that I might enjoy
> The wealth of Your creation.
> You were punished
> For all my mistakes
> So I'd be declared not guilty
> By association.
> You took all that I am heir to
> And gave me all that belonged to You.
> What more could anyone do?

When I accepted You I never realized
That I'd be accepted, too.
It took awhile to see
That You bore God's rejection
So He'd never turn away from me.
I never knew I would receive so much
When I accepted You.

You met death
So that I might know life
And eternal restoration.
You took on the world
So the likeness of God
Could be drawn on my being
Like a blood relation.
The deepest needs my lifetime through
Were all met on the cross by You.
What more could anyone do?

You are the adopted son or daughter of God, who is the Creator of all and King of the universe. This means you are royalty. Jesus sacrificed His life for you to wear the helmet of salvation, which is like a crown on your head distinguishing you as regal. We put on the helmet of salvation the moment we receive the Lord, but we must constantly remember what Jesus saved us *for* and *from* and who we are in Him. We should never minimize what that means in any way. Receiving Jesus gives us so much more than we can even begin to realize at the time we make that commitment to Him.

Put on the helmet of salvation every day by reminding yourself of what Jesus did for you and why you now have the right to wear it as a royal crown.

Take the Sword of the Spirit, Which Is the Word of God

Satan tried to destroy Jesus when He was born by inspiring wicked King Herod to kill all the babies in Bethlehem. Thirty years later, when Jesus was baptized and led into the wilderness by the Holy Spirit, Satan attacked Him again. Jesus' weapon against him was God's Word—which is the "sword of the Spirit."

No spiritual battle can be fought and won without our greatest weapon—the Word of God.

God's Word was inspired by the Holy Spirit. It is God breathed. Each writer of the Bible was moved by the Spirit as his gifts and intellect were used by God to speak *to* them and *through* them. The Word of God is so powerful that *it is a double-edged sword in our hands* (Hebrews 4:12). That means it is a *defensive* as well as *offensive* weapon. As prayer warriors, we need both.

Once you receive the Lord, the Holy Spirit in you brings the Word alive to your mind, soul, and spirit every time you read it. Some people say, "This part of the Bible was only for the Old Testament people, and that part was only for the disciples, and that other part was only for the Ephesians, and this was only for the Philippians," and on and on until the entire Bible is explained away as just a history book. *Beware of anyone who wants to make the Bible into just a history book.* The Bible is alive. It is living and it has power for today. "All Scripture is given by inspiration of God, and is profitable for doctrine, for reproof, for correction, for instruction in righteousness, *that the man of God may be complete, thoroughly equipped for every good work*" (2 Timothy 3:16-17).

I feel I must say here that when the Bible says something like "man of God" as it does in the verses quoted above, it is not excluding women. It's like saying "mankind." And we all know that word includes women as well. So if you are a woman, don't become concerned about that. Believe me, I have heard as many concerns from men having a hard time over being called "the bride of Christ."

Every time you read God's Word, it will become more firmly planted in your mind and heart. From there it will protect you from attacks of the enemy. The next chapter, "Become Skilled with Your Spiritual Weapons," contains information about how to use God's Word as a weapon against the enemy the way Jesus did. For now, put on the Word like a protective garment every morning. *Speak the word, pray the Word, live the Word, and let it live in you* so it becomes part of your armor.

Pray Always with All Prayer and Supplication in the Spirit

God wants us to be persistent in our praying. That's what it means to pray without ceasing. It is not intermittent start-and-stop-whenever-I-am-desperate kind of praying. It is deliberate. It is with knowledge of what we are doing and why. It is not random throw-it-up-and-see-if-it-sticks kind of praying. It's praying always, with every kind of prayer and supplication in the Spirit, which means it is Holy Spirit ignited.

Praying always means praying through things and not giving up. It means being ever-watchful and persevering in prayer in order to see breakthrough.

It is important to pray according to the will of God. "*If we ask anything according to His will*, He hears us" (1 John 5:14). The way to do that is to pray with the Word of God woven into our heart and our prayers. "If you abide in Me, and *My words abide in you*, you will ask what you desire, and it shall be done for you" (John 15:7). And it is to pray with the leading of the Spirit.

After Jesus taught His disciples to pray what we call the Lord's Prayer, He said, "Which of you shall have a friend, and go to him at midnight and say to him, 'Friend, lend me three loaves; for a friend of mine has come to me on his journey, and I have nothing to set before him'; and he will answer from within and say, 'Do not trouble me; the door is now shut, and my children are with me in bed; I cannot rise and give to you'? I say to you, though he will not rise and give to him because he is his friend, yet *because of his persistence he will rise and give him as many as he needs*" (Luke 11:5-8).

Jesus is saying keep asking.

Jesus said, "So I say to you, *ask*, and it will be *given* to you; *seek*, and you will *find*; *knock*, and it will be *opened* to you. For *everyone who asks receives*, and *he who seeks finds*, and *to him who knocks it will be opened*" (Luke 11:9-10).

Jesus is saying keep praying.

Be Watchful to the End

When a soldier is on active duty, he sleeps in his battle gear. He doesn't put on his jammies and fuzzy slippers while he is on the battlefield. He stays dressed in case of a surprise attack. We do the same. We don't take our armor off when we go to bed at night. It is protecting us while we sleep. But in the morning we need to put it on fresh and new—polished, so to speak—so that we have maximum protection for the day.

Part of our protective armor is our own praying. I have told people this in my prayer groups for years, and they have felt it and observed it. That is, there is a blessing for us when we are praying. Although this is not something we expect, great rewards are given to us when we pray in response to the call of God on our lives. The now-and-then praying doesn't do that. It is the everyday, consistent praying that seems to build up rewards for us in a holy bank in heaven. We keep making deposits, and when we need to make a big withdrawal on earth, we have enough to cover it. I cannot prove this to you, but I know from experience that it's true. Try praying frequently and consistently and see if it doesn't prove true for you too. The more you pray, the more answers to prayer you will see.

Our prayers are not answered as a way of rewarding us for good behavior, like a child who is promised an ice-cream cone if he behaves in the grocery store. Our obedience to God is evidence that we are in alignment with His will. The most important thing is not to get what *we* want in prayer, but to accomplish what *God* wants. We delight ourselves in Him first. We make Him our priority and our greatest desire is to please Him. "Delight yourself also in the LORD, and He shall give you the desires of your heart" (Psalm 37:4).

When we delight ourselves in Him and listen for His Holy Spirit to guide us as we pray, powerful things happen.

Prayer for the Prayer Warrior

Lord, help me to put on the full spiritual armor You have provided for me so that I can "stand against the wiles of the devil" every day. Show me how to gird up the core of my being with Your truth so that I don't fall into deception of any kind. Teach me to not only *know* Your truth, but to *live* in it. Help me to put on the breastplate of righteousness that protects me from the enemy's attacks. I know it is Your righteousness *in* me that protects me, but I also know I must not neglect to put on Your righteousness like a bulletproof vest by doing what is right in Your eyes. Reveal to me thoughts, attitudes, and habits of my heart that are not pleasing to You. Show me what I have done, or am *about* to do, that does not glorify You. I want to see anything in me that violates Your high standards for my life so I can confess it, turn away from it, and be cleansed from all unrighteousness.

Thank You, Jesus, that I have peace beyond comprehension because of what You accomplished on the cross for me. Help me to stand secure with my feet protected by the good news that You have already prepared and secured for me. Because I have peace *with* You and *from* You, I am able to not only stand strong but to walk forward against the enemy and take back territory he has stolen from us all.

Thank You that You have given me faith and have grown my faith in Your Word. I don't have faith in my own faith, as if I have accomplished anything myself, but I have faith in You and Your faithfulness to me, which is a shield from the enemy's arrows. Just as You were Abraham's shield and

David's shield, You are mine as well. Thank You that even if my faith is shaky one day, Your faithfulness never is. "O LORD of hosts, blessed is the man who trusts in You!" (Psalm 84:12). Help me to remember Your faithfulness at all times. You, Lord, are "my strength and my shield"; my heart trusts in You "and I am helped" (Psalm 28:7). Enable me to take up the shield of faith as constant protection from the enemy. My soul waits for You, Lord, my help and my shield (Psalm 33:20).

Help me to put on the helmet of salvation to protect my head and mind each day by remembering all You have saved me from, including the lies of the enemy. Enable me to remember only what *You* say about me and not what the enemy wants me to believe. Thank You that Your helmet of salvation protects me from warfare in my mind. Your salvation gives me everything I need in order to live successfully.

Help me to take up the sword of the Spirit every day, for Your Word not only *protects* me from the enemy, but it is my greatest *weapon* against him. Enable me to always pray as Your Spirit leads me, and to keep on praying as long as I should. Teach me to be the strong and unshakeable prayer warrior You want me to be so I can accomplish Your will.

In Jesus' name I pray.

> *The night is far spent, the day is at hand.*
> *Therefore let us cast off the works of darkness,*
> *and let us put on the armor of light.*
>
> ROMANS 13:12

7

Become Skilled with Your Spiritual Weapons

Just as a soldier trains diligently with his weapons so he can do well in battle, we also must train with our spiritual weapons in order to do well in every battle *we* face. When Navy SEALs go on assignment, each one not only carries his main weapon, which is a powerful automatic rifle, but he also has other weapons, such as a small gun, a knife or two, explosives, plenty of ammunition, and other specific and key items that give him an advantage over the enemy.

Before each assignment, SEALs check their weapons thoroughly to make sure they have precisely the right ones for what they are about to do. They know their weapons well and are so highly skilled that using them has become second nature. They practice with them until they never miss because they can't afford to make a mistake. We, too, must become so familiar and skilled with our spiritual weapons that functioning in them becomes second nature to us. We can't afford to do otherwise.

Our Main Weapon Is the Sword of the Spirit

As prayer warriors in God's army, we must train with our main weapon, which is the Word of God. It is not only part of our *protective* armor, but also a powerful *weapon* as well. It is highly accurate, and if you are knowledgeable as to how to handle it as a weapon against the enemy, it is unfailing. If you aim correctly, it hits the target dead-on every time. The more skilled you are at using this powerful weapon, the greater advantage you will have. In fact, the enemy cannot stand against it.

No soldier *resists* the enemy without his weapon. Neither does a soldier ever *attack* his enemy without the weapon he knows best how to use. He understands its capabilities, is completely familiar with it, and has practiced with it countless times. A soldier's weapons are always kept up to the highest standard and ready to use. We must do the same. We cannot wait until the enemy attacks to become familiar with our spiritual weapons; we have to know each weapon now so we are prepared for anything. The Word of God is our best weapon because it will always be exactly what we need in order to face every threat.

God is unchanging. That's because He doesn't *need* to change. He is perfect and complete. And His Word is the same. The sword of the Spirit is never irrelevant, no matter how much the enemy tries to make it seem that way. That's why you can claim promises in the Bible as absolute truth for your life. When Jesus was tempted by the enemy in the wilderness, He resisted with Scripture specifically aimed at thwarting the enemy's temptations. Even the enemy knows that the Word of God is powerful and unfailing and he can never prevail against it. That's why he finally left Jesus alone. He could not trick *Him* the way he can with far too many of *us*.

Our faith is extremely important in the effectiveness of this main weapon. And the more we train and practice in our knowledge and retention of the Word, the more our faith develops. The more diligently we *read* the Word, *quote* the Word, *pray* the Word, and *do* the Word, the stronger our faith will be. Our greatest weapon—God's Word—mixed with our faith will prove to be the invincible weapon we need in every situation.

When marksmen or snipers train, they do it full-time. They make practicing with their weapon a way of life so that it becomes part of who they are. In the missions they are sent on they cannot afford to miss. They have to be dead-on every time. In that same way, our greatest weapon—the Word of God—must become part of who *we* are and not just something we read or hear. We must pore over it, read *all* of it, understand it, and be able to stay solid in everything we know of it. That takes practice.

That's why it is important to read the Bible every day. Ask the Holy Spirit to make whatever you are reading that day come alive in a new and deeper way in you. The Holy Spirit will meet you there on the page and do exactly that. It's also crucial to have some verses etched in your memory so that you can draw on them whenever you need to. If you have not done that before, start with just one. For example, I have put four verses below. Take one and read it over and over for a week. Write it down on a piece of paper or card and carry it with you. Tape it to your mirror or refrigerator or wherever your eyes will often see it. Say it. Proclaim it. Make it become part of you. When you feel it is solid in you, add the next one and do the same. I guarantee you will need these Scriptures for the rest of your life. And you will definitely want them clear and strong in your mind and heart when you pray.

Week 1: "If God is for us, who can be against us?" (Romans 8:31).

Week 2: "God has not given us a spirit of fear, but of power and of love and of a sound mind" (2 Timothy 1:7).

Week 3: "Do not be conformed to this world, but be transformed by the renewing of your mind, that you may prove what is that good and acceptable and perfect will of God" (Romans 12:2).

Week 4: "Be anxious for nothing, but in everything by prayer and supplication, with thanksgiving, let your requests be made known to God; and the peace of God, which surpasses all understanding, will guard your hearts and minds through Christ Jesus" (Philippians 4:6-7).

(You will find more to choose from after each prayer in chapter 12, "Pray the Prayers Every Prayer Warrior Must Know.")

Scripture memorization is not something to wear as a badge of honor and self-satisfaction, or to beat yourself up over if you haven't done it. Rather, it is to be viewed as an instrument of survival and warfare. First of all, it keeps you from doing the wrong thing. "Your word I have hidden in my heart, that I might not sin against You" (Psalm 119:11). And it gives you an unshakeable foundation when you face difficult situations. "Great peace have those who love Your law, and nothing causes them to stumble" (Psalm 119:165).

Having Scripture etched on your heart should never be an overwhelming challenge that in any way causes you discouragement. It should be a joy and not a burden. You don't have to memorize the entire Bible or even a book or a chapter. Of course, it's great if you can do that, but as a prayer warrior you must have key verses that become so much a part of you that you can speak them the moment you need them. Don't think of it as memorization. Think of it as saying something so many times it is engraved on your brain and heart.

Don't look at this as too much work. It's no more work than eating. This is *feeding your spirit* and *anchoring your soul* with something that will nourish you, strengthen you, protect you, and change your life. This is a crucial part of the living relationship you have with God through Jesus, His Son, and His Holy Spirit in you, who guides you day by day and moment by moment. Let it become part of your life as naturally as drinking water or brushing your teeth. When you read God's Word and say it often enough, it will become just like a soldier's weapon. If you did that with one verse a week or even a month, you would have a lot more of the Word etched on your mind and heart than most people will in a lifetime. You will be amazed at the strength and security you feel when you are armed properly.

Every time you read the Word of God it will become more and more entrenched in your heart—no matter how many times you have read it before. When you speak the Word of God in the face of every attack of the enemy, you are driving a sword through his plans. Although the Bible calls the Word of God the sword of the Spirit, we must not wield it like a weapon against people. We must always remember who our real enemy is. It is always used most effectively against the enemy. With people, we speak God's Word to encourage, uplift, direct, free, advise, inform, strengthen, and lovingly affirm them.

The Word will change us every time we read it. If it has no effect in us and we don't actually *live* the Word, then our prayers will not have power. If we speak it and don't believe it—or read it and don't live it—it won't have the life-changing effect in our hearts that it could. But there is no way it won't affect us if we are *seeking to hear* from God on its pages.

Don't get me wrong. The Word of God is powerful in and of itself to transform lives and situations, but people who have no faith in God or His Word cannot direct it in prayer and see it penetrate situations with impact. You can't just say, "Here's a verse I am throwing out there. I don't know what it means and I don't really believe it, but it's worth a try." There is no power there. If Jesus Himself— the Son of God—could not do miracles in the presence of unbelief, how much less can we do them in the presence of our *own* unbelief?

Every time you read God's Word, it should inspire prayer either for yourself, someone else, or some situation you know about. When you're praying, include the Word in your prayers. God's Word is never ineffective. He says of His Word, "As rain comes down, and the snow from heaven, and do not return there, but water the earth, and make it bring forth and bud, that it may give seed to the sower and bread to the eater, so shall My word be that goes forth from My mouth; *it shall not return to Me void*, but it shall accomplish what I please, *and it shall prosper in the thing for which I sent it*" (Isaiah 55:10-11). We need the Word to water and feed our soul, and God promises it will produce beyond what we dream possible.

Worship Is a Powerful Weapon Against the Enemy

After we put on our protective armor—truth, righteousness, the gospel of peace, faith, salvation, and the sword of the Spirit—there are other powerful weapons God has given us against the enemy that we must become skilled with as well. One extremely powerful weapon is praise and worship.

The enemy despises our worship and praise to God so much that he cannot even be in the presence of anyone who is actively doing that. So whenever you want the enemy to flee, worship God. It is one of our greatest weapons in the war against him. And it is our correct response to God for all He has done and is doing in our lives.

Praise is called a sacrifice because we sacrifice our time and self-focus in order to direct our attention to the Lord. When we worship God, we lay down whatever consumes us and become consumed with *Him*. Praise and worship take the focus off of ourselves and put it entirely on God. We fully recognize Jesus as everything and praise Him for everything He *is* and has *done* for us. We worship Him for His blood sacrifice for us on the cross, and praise Him for His love demonstrated to us in that He willingly laid down His life so we could live with Him forever. We praise Him for His forgiveness of all our sins so that we are never again separated from God.

We praise Him for the gift of life He has secured for us and the countless other wonderful things He has given us. We worship Him for all that He is—God, Lord, Savior, Deliverer, Healer, Provider, Protector, and much more. In other words, we never lack a reason to worship and praise God.

If prayer in its simplest form is communicating with God, then praise and worship is the purest form of prayer.

Paul told the Ephesians to walk wisely because the days were evil and they needed to always understand what the will of God was for them (Ephesians 5:15-16). Doesn't that sound like today? Right now? Are not the days evil? Do we not desperately need to know God's will in all we do? Paul told them, "Do not be drunk with wine, in which is dissipation; *but be filled with the Spirit*, speaking to one another in psalms and hymns and spiritual songs, *singing and making melody in your heart to the Lord"* (Ephesians 5:18-19*)*.

Being filled with the Spirit is not a onetime thing. The verb here implies that we need to be *continually filled*. That doesn't mean that the Holy Spirit runs out or dissipates in you. It means that we need to be filled *afresh* with more of what God has for us. It implies we have a choice. What are we open to? Rather than being filled with temporary things, we must be filled with that which is eternal—a well that never runs dry. When we are filled afresh each day with the Holy Spirit, our worship never runs dry either. It can't.

One of the greatest things about praise and worship—and the very reason they are so powerful—is that when we worship God, He inhabits our praise.

When you worship God, His presence comes to be with you in greater power. No wonder the enemy can't stay around. The Bible says, "The Lord is the Spirit; and *where the Spirit of the Lord is, there is liberty"* (2 Corinthians 3:17). Isn't that the best news? It means in the presence of the Holy Spirit we are liberated. Jesus gives you the Holy Spirit when you receive Him, but the Holy Spirit waits for your invitation to *manifest* in greater ways in your life. Your worship is that invitation. In response to it, He comes to live in you in even greater measure and power.

Paul goes on to say, "We all, with unveiled face, beholding as in a mirror the glory of the Lord, are *being transformed into the same image from glory to glory*, just as by the Spirit of the Lord" (2 Corinthians 3:18). Whenever we worship the Lord, we are going from glory to glory. We are being transformed. The more we worship Him, the more we see Him reflected in us. The truth is we reflect what we behold. The more we look to Jesus in worship, the more we are transformed into His image by the power of His Spirit.

When you train diligently with your spiritual weapons, it means you use them so often that when the enemy attacks, you automatically revert to what you know. That's why you must remember to *worship God the minute you sense an enemy attack.*

The enemy hates your worship of God because his own greatest objective is to get you to worship him instead.

Don't react to an enemy attack with doubt, fear, or lack of understanding about spiritual things. Do what you've been trained to do because it is second nature to you. That means immediately lift up praise to the Lord, proclaiming His power over evil. Worship Him as Lord over your life and your circumstances.

God wants us to present our *whole* selves to Him in worship. "I beseech you therefore, brethren, by the mercies of God, that you *present your bodies a living sacrifice, holy, acceptable to God, which is your reasonable service*" (Romans 12:1). When you wake up every day, give yourself and your day to the Lord. Choose to have a heart of thanksgiving, praise, and worship. Thank God for the day. Praise Him for everything you are grateful for. Worship Him for Who He is. If you do not praise and worship God daily, you are not prepared for *anything.* When worship and praise come automatically, you are prepared for *everything* the enemy will throw at you.

Paul said, "*Rejoice in the Lord always. Again I will say, rejoice!*" (Philippians 4:4). "Let us *continually offer the sacrifice of praise* to God, that is, the fruit of our lips, giving thanks to His name" (Hebrews 13:15). That means praise should be ongoing and continual.

There is nothing more powerful than worship of God. It can shake things up in the spirit realm and in our lives like nothing else can. It causes chains to fall off of people. Paul and Silas were in prison for their faith in Jesus, but instead of complaining and questioning God as to why they were there, they were "praying and singing hymns to God, and the prisoners were listening to them. *Suddenly there was a great earthquake, so that the foundations of the prison were shaken; and immediately all the doors were opened and everyone's chains were loosed*" (Acts 16:25-26).

Now that's the kind of earthquake we want—the kind that breaks chains and sets captives free.

God's Grace Is a Weapon Against the Enemy

Grace is the unmerited favor of God. When the apostles witnessed the resurrection of Jesus, they experienced the power of God and "grace was upon them all" (Acts 4:33). *Grace also means the operations of God's power.* God not only saves us by grace, but He also gives us His Holy Spirit, whose power is at work in us by God's grace as well. We don't deserve God's grace and power, but because of what Jesus accomplished on the cross we are given those gifts.

Zechariah the prophet gave a word from God to Zerubbabel (pronounced Zer-rubb'-a-bul), who was the governor of Judah and responsible for rebuilding the temple. Zechariah said that the rebuilding would not be accomplished by human power or the force of an army, but by God's Holy Spirit empowering them. God said it would happen *"not by might nor by power, but by My Spirit"* (Zechariah 4:6).

God then instructed Zerubbabel to speak grace to the mountain—the mountain being the hindrance of Satan who opposed anyone trying to rebuild the temple. The Lord went on to say, "Who are you, O great mountain? Before Zerubbabel you shall become a plain! And he shall bring forth the capstone with *shouts of 'Grace, grace to it!'"* (Zechariah 4:7). In other words, the rebuilding of the temple would happen not because of human strength or ability, but because of the grace of God. Zerubbabel was to *speak the grace of God to the situation.*

That is a powerful lesson to us all, and we must not forget it.

We, too, can speak "grace" to our mountain of obstacles. We can speak the Word of God in faith and invite the Holy Spirit to operate in power through us as we pray. And then, when we are certain what God's will is, we can speak "grace" to the seemingly insurmountable enemy opposition. And the enemy will have no power against it, because he can't tell us we don't deserve God's grace. We already know that. He cannot tell us that we are not powerful enough to make it happen on our own. We already know that too. All we need to know is that *God* is powerful and full of grace, and *He* will make it happen.

There will be many times when the opposition from the enemy to the thing you are praying for seems as monumental and immovable as a mountain. When that happens, speak grace to that spiritual mountain. If you are in a place where you can *shout* grace, say, "Lord, I shout *grace* to this mountain. Bring it down so it has no power." Remember that God said to Zerubbabel that the rebuilding of the temple would not be done by human strength, but by His Holy Spirit. It is the same for the mountain *you* are facing. Invite the Holy Spirit to work a miracle in your situation. Speak God's grace to any immoveable mountain the enemy puts in front of you. *The enemy can never stand against what God desires to do by His grace.*

Fasting with Prayer Is a Weapon Against the Enemy

In the Bible, people fasted and prayed before they made important decisions. Paul did amazing signs and wonders while the church fasted and prayed. People were sent out into ministry after fasting and praying. Esther called the Jews to fast and pray to save their people from annihilation. Fasting breaks down the plans of the enemy and accomplishes God's will.

Because spiritual warfare is continuous, we must pray continually. Jesus' disciples were determined to make prayer and teaching the Word a priority. They said, "We will *give ourselves continually to prayer* and to the ministry of the word" (Acts 6:4). That must be *our priority* as well. But our praying can increase in power when we also *fast along* with praying. Fasting is a formidable weapon against the enemy in order to see strongholds broken and breakthrough happen.

Fasting can "loose the bonds of wickedness," "undo heavy burdens," "let the oppressed go free," "break every yoke," and much more (Isaiah 58:6). Read Isaiah 58:6-14 to see what all the Lord will do when you fast. It will inspire and encourage you. A fast doesn't have to be beyond what you can handle. A 24-hour fast is powerful and effective. Even fasting one meal or two and praying instead can accomplish great breakthrough. I know that may not seem like much to you, and you may think, *How can that be enough to accomplish anything?* But it can. I have seen it countless times in my own life and in the lives of others.

Fasting and prayer is a powerful weapon against the enemy. So when you need a breakthrough in any area of your life, fast and pray and see what God does in response. Some things will not happen without it.

Faith Is Not Only a Shield; It Is a Weapon

We cannot do anything without faith—especially please God. "*Without faith it is impossible to please Him,* for he who comes to God must believe that He is, and that He is a rewarder of those who diligently seek Him" (Hebrews 11:6). Having faith in God is the opposite of trusting in ourselves. Faith means being convinced that God will do as He promised, so we stop striving to do everything on our own.

The Bible says of Abraham's faith that he was certain God would do what He said He would. "Being fully convinced that what He had promised He was also able to perform. And therefore it was accounted to him for righteousness" (Romans 4:21-22). Having that same certainty about God not only *shields* us from the enemy but *defeats* him as well.

Our strong faith not only serves as our protective shield, but it is also one of our powerful weapons against the enemy.

We must have faith that God hears and will answer our prayers. Jesus said, "Have faith in God. For assuredly, I say to you, *whoever says to this mountain, 'Be removed and be cast into the sea,'* and does not doubt in his heart, but believes that those things he says will be done, *he will have whatever he says.* Therefore I say to you, *whatever things you ask when you pray, believe that you receive them, and you will have them*" (Mark 11:22-24). This doesn't mean we tell God what to do. We don't dictate the way or timing of how God answers our prayers. *We don't have faith in our faith so that we think we control things with our faith.* We are not going to force God to do anything that is not His will.

Something happens every time we pray, but we cannot put limits on what we think God can or will do, because the answer is up to Him.

Ask God for the strength to bear up under difficult circumstances with hope in your heart and faith that does not waiver, even in the midst of a storm. The Bible says, *"Let him ask in faith, with no doubting,* for he who doubts is like a wave of the sea driven and tossed by the wind. For let not that man suppose that he will receive anything from the Lord" (James 1:6-7). When you live by faith, you persevere through any opposition.

The Bible says, *"The just shall live by faith*; but if anyone draws back, My soul has no pleasure in him" (Hebrews 10:38). It says we should stand strong in faith, because *"faith is the substance of things hoped for, the evidence of things not seen"* (Hebrews 11:1).

Sarah did the impossible. She conceived and gave birth to a child when she was ninety years old, well past the time when a woman is able to do that. This happened because she believed God and knew He was faithful to do what He said He would (Hebrews 11:11). She did not look at her own inabilities but instead dwelled on the ability of God to do the impossible. We, too, need to have the kind of faith that believes God can do the impossible when we pray.

We need to stop looking at our own impossibilities, and instead look to the God of the impossible in faith.

Steadfast faith means we believe 100 percent in God and His Word whether we see every prayer answered the way we want or not.

Whether you see everything you ask for come to pass should not be the determining factor in the strength of your faith or your attitude toward God. Your steadfast walk of faith has to do simply with your believing God. Every day proclaim in your heart that Jesus is Lord of your life and you have absolute faith in Him. Then, no matter what is happening in and around you, your faith becomes a weapon against the enemy.

A soldier does not question his commander or decide not to follow his orders. He doesn't have the privilege of sitting in judgment on his commander or what he is required to do. And neither do we. The Bible says that, "No one engaged in warfare entangles himself with the affairs of this life, that he may please him who enlisted him as a soldier" (2 Timothy 2:4). That means every good soldier strictly obeys his commander without questions coming from his or her flesh. As a prayer warrior, you and I must listen to and obey our Commander, and not judge His decisions—His answers to our prayers. Trusting God means we obey Him without question. *That* is strong faith. And it is not only a shield, but also a weapon that destroys the work of the enemy.

Prayer Is Always a Powerful Weapon Against the Enemy

While prayer is the battle itself, it is also a weapon. In prayer we tell God what we want Him to do. It's not that He is unaware of the problem or doesn't know what is going on. He knows what is going to happen before it happens. Before we see the need, He already knows the answer. "It shall come to pass that *before they call, I will answer*; and while *they are still speaking, I will hear*" (Isaiah 65:24).

God has set it up that *we pray* and *He answers*. He doesn't make us robots. He doesn't impose His will on us. He waits for us to choose *His* will over our own. The reason He does this is so we will walk with Him in an ever-deepening relationship.

Right now He is using whatever difficult situations you have in your life to draw you closer to Him in prayer, in His Word, and in worship. He wants you to depend on Him because He desires to take you to places you cannot get to without Him. You can't get there from here without His help. He wants to make you whole and strong in a way you could never be without Him. He wants to teach you things you will not understand apart from His Spirit in you.

What God wants to do *in* you, *through* you, and *for* you is more than you can imagine. "Eye has not seen, nor ear heard, nor have entered into the heart of man the things which God has prepared for those who love Him. But God has revealed them to us through His Spirit. For the Spirit searches all things, yes, the deep things of God" (1 Corinthians 2:9-10).

Imitate Jesus when you pray. He viewed praying as communion with His heavenly Father. It wasn't a duty. It was a need.

Jesus prayed first thing in the morning. "In the morning, having risen a long while before daylight, He went out and departed to a solitary place; and there He prayed" (Mark 1:35).

Jesus prayed at night. "He went out to the mountain to pray, and continued all night in prayer to God" (Luke 6:12).

Jesus prayed alone. "When He had sent the multitudes away, He went up on the mountain by Himself to pray. Now when evening came, He was alone there" (Matthew 14:23).

Jesus prayed without ceasing. "*Watch therefore, and pray always* that you may be counted worthy to escape all these things that will come to pass, and to stand before the Son of Man" (Luke 21:36).

Jesus could do nothing without praying. "The Son can do nothing of Himself, but what He sees the Father do; for whatever He does, the Son also does in like manner" (John 5:19).

We need to pray as Jesus did—day and night, without ceasing, in private communion with God.

When you bring your concerns and needs to the Lord and ask Him to meet those needs, that is called petitionary praying. When you petition God for something, don't stop praying. Bring it to Him again and again if you need to until you have peace in your heart that you have truly left it in His hands. After each prayer, thank Him that He has heard your prayers and that He will answer in His way and in His time.

God is very specific about what He wants from us. You must be specific too. As you pray, tell God that above all you want His will to be done. Because if you are praying for something that is *not* His will, you want to know it and be led by His Spirit to pray the right thing. Do not sit in judgment on how well you think you prayed. That is not your job. Your work is to pray. It is God's work to answer the way He wants to. And definitely do not sit in judgment on how God has answered unless you are fond of lightning. You simply pray and leave the outcome in God's hands to answer in His way and time. Then every time you pray, your prayers will become a weapon against the enemy and his plans for your life.

Prayer for the
Prayer Warrior

Lord, help me to understand what my spiritual weapons are and to become proficient in the use of them. Teach me so I don't forget for even a moment how powerful they are. Grow my faith to believe You and Your Word without doubt. I know that as the heavens are higher than the earth, so are Your ways higher than my ways, and Your thoughts higher than my thoughts (Isaiah 55:9). Help me to think and act more like You every time I read Your Word and spend time in Your presence. Enable me to know Your Word so well that I have Scriptures in my mind and heart that become automatic weapons against the enemy of my soul.

Thank You for Your grace toward me, rewarding and helping me beyond what I deserve. When I face a mountain of opposition by the enemy, remind me to speak grace to that situation. I know that Your grace overrides any plan of the enemy no matter how much he appears to be succeeding. Help me not to be intimidated by the enemy's force when the force of Your grace far exceeds any efforts of his.

Show me whenever I need to fast along with praying in order to accomplish all You want to see done. Enable me to do it. Help me to fully understand all You have said in Your Word about what will be accomplished during a fast. I know that in obedience to You, a fast will undo heavy burdens, let the oppressed go free, and break every yoke (Isaiah 58:6).

I worship You, Lord, above all things. Help me to worship You "in spirit and truth" as Your Word says to do (John 4:24). I seek after You and long for You, just as a "deer pants for the water brooks" (Psalm 42:1). Help me to make praise and worship my *first* reaction to things that happen and the different situations that present themselves to me.

Lord, You have said, "Ask, and it will be given to you; seek, and you will find; knock, and it will be opened to you. For everyone who asks receives, and he who seeks finds, and to him who knocks it will be opened" (Luke 11:9-10). Help me to ask according to Your leading, seek to understand Your will, and knock on the doors You want opened. Enable me to keep asking, keep seeking, and keep knocking and not give up. Remind me how these actions are weapons against the plans of the enemy so that only *Your* plans for my life and the lives of the people for whom I pray will be done. I thank You in advance for Your answers to my prayers.

Thank You that You are "able to do exceedingly abundantly above all that we ask or think, according to the power that works in us" (Ephesians 3:20). Thank You that no weapon formed against me or the people for whom I pray will ever prosper.

In Jesus' name I pray.

No weapon formed against you shall prosper,
and every tongue which rises against you in
judgment You shall condemn.
"This is the heritage of the servants of the Lord,
and their righteousness is from Me," says the Lord.

Isaiah 54:17

8

Engage in the War Knowing Time Is Short

It is one thing to put on our *spiritual armor* and take up our *spiritual weapons,* but it is another to actually make the decision to *engage in the war* and *go to battle in prayer.* It is not good enough to *think* about prayer, *talk* about prayer, or *read* about prayer. You have to *pray.* Soldiers can *prepare* for battle, *learn* about battle, *train* for battle, and have the best equipment in the world, but if they never go to battle against the enemy, the enemy wins.

Each one of us has to get the vision about being a prayer warrior. We are a large and mighty group, but not near as large and mighty as God wants us to be. God calls us *all* to pray. Jesus taught us about *prayer.* He told us *what* to do when we pray, and *how* to pray. We can memorize everything the Bible says about prayer, but if we are not praying, God's will is not being done, and the enemy is advancing instead of the kingdom of God.

You don't have to *enlist* in the army because you have already enlisted when you receive the Lord, but you do have to *engage.* The battles are not becoming less frequent or less intense with time; they are increasing in every way. We cannot ignore that fact and expect to remain standing.

We must engage in the war *now* because the enemy knows he has only a short time before the return of the Lord, and he is letting out all the stops. The war against believers is pushed into overdrive. We can see the incessant attacks on the health, emotions, relationships, work, reputations, finances, and safety of every believer. They are epidemic and we cannot ignore them.

"Engage" means to *pledge. To promise. To give an oath.* To *pledge one's word* to assume an obligation. To *enter into conflict.* It also means to bring troops into conflict. "Engage" means choosing to involve oneself or commit oneself to something. It means you have pledged to be involved in entering into conflict. It means you recognize that a war is going on and you understand God is calling you to pray.

With regard to being a prayer warrior, "engage" means to pledge to God that you are choosing to oppose the plans of the enemy by praying for God's will to be done on earth.

I have not talked in my books about being a prayer warrior before because I saw how many people struggled with simple prayers for themselves and their loved ones. They needed a reliable and consistent way to bring their needs before God and not wait until they became desperate prayers. But more and more, as I have had people come up to me wherever I am and told me they are a prayer warrior too, I know firsthand that an army of you is out there that is far greater than most of us realize.

We see that the world is growing darker day by day as evil is exalted and spreading like a wildfire. That's why our army of prayer warriors must increase in numbers and strength. I am asking you to please join our ranks if you have not already. If you have put your faith in Jesus, and you have a heart for God and His ways, and you are grateful for the leading of His Holy Spirit in your life, then you can do this. I hope I have convinced you by now, but if not, then the rest of this book surely will.

I am asking you to recognize who you are in the Lord, what He has done for you, and what He has called you to do. You are not weak. You are a child of the King, and He is strong in you by the power of His Spirit. You have a high calling on your life that has nothing to do with gender, age, accomplishment, education level, race, culture, color, political party, or blood type. We are all children of God under one blood—the blood of Christ. He has called you to put on the whole armor of God and engage in the war. You are never alone in the battle, and that is great comfort. There are '"ministering spirits sent forth to minister for those who will inherit salvation" (Hebrews 1:14). That's you and me. We have an inheritance in the Lord. There are angels, who help us. There is the Holy Spirit, who is *in* us and *enables* us.

There have been countless people before us who felt as we do in the face of enemy opposition, yet they fought the enemy with courage because they knew he was *God's* enemy too, and God is the ultimate victor. We may not receive recognition as a great prayer warrior on earth, but God knows our efforts in prayer. He says in the book of Revelation that *in heaven are "golden bowls full of incense, which are the prayers of the saints"* (Revelation 5:8). Can it be that when we pray, our prayers don't just evaporate into thin air? They last? That means when we pray, our prayers don't just have a shelf life of a few seconds. They live on. They exist before God and continue to accomplish His will. How great is that? What we do as prayer warriors lasts even beyond our lifetime.

I believe that the prayer you pray today doesn't just fall to the ground without ever reaching above the ceiling. I believe your prayer for salvation for someone today can have an effect even after you have gone to be with the Lord. You never know how your prayer may be answered for that person on their deathbed. You don't know. Only God does.

However, we can't always be putting out fires. We also have to be preventing them. We have to be proactive and pray in anticipation of the enemy's tactics. We must pray prayers of protection from the enemy for ourselves, our families, and all the people whom God puts on our heart. But first we have to deliberately engage in the war.

Engage Because You Don't Know All That Your Prayers May Accomplish

We prayer warriors don't receive much credit for our labor from people who are not prayer warriors themselves, but we have the great reward of seeing God move in response to our prayers.

In the church I attended in Los Angeles, a band of us prayer warriors prayed on Wednesday nights. We had a deep burden for the people of East Berlin at the time, who lived in terrible poverty of body, soul, and spirit behind the Berlin Wall, which was erected by the Russians to keep people from crossing over into freedom. We believed we were being led by the Holy Spirit to pray for that wall to come down. We knew we were probably not the only ones praying, but because we had such a burden for that situation we prayed as if we were. We prayed with a mission because we knew we were on assignment from God. None of us could even imagine how that wall could possibly come down, but we prayed anyway. And years later it did. I do not believe for a moment that the Berlin Wall just came down on that one day. I believe with all my heart that the wall was brought down in the spirit realm first in the years preceding it. That battle was won in prayer. The forces of evil that erected the wall in the first place, forcing people into isolation, poverty, cruelty, and separation from loved ones, depriving them of freedom, food, work, and the necessities for any quality of life, were defeated in prayer first.

Years later someone who knew of what I had been a part of and had actually been there when the wall was torn down, brought me a piece of the Berlin Wall. I have it on a shelf. And it is a constant reminder to me that we don't know the power of our prayers. Even when we don't have enough faith to believe wholeheartedly for what we are praying, God is faithful to keep His promise to hear our prayers and answer. I did not have enough faith to believe that wall would come down, but I had faith that the God of the impossible could do anything He willed to do if He could just find enough people to go to battle for Him against the enemy in prayer.

You might think there is no immediate benefit to you if you are praying for other people or situations in other places, but that's not true. As long as you are praying, you are receiving blessings from God that might not be there if you were not praying. First of all, you are drawing close to God, and that is always a good thing. Being with the Lord is a reward in itself. I know you are not praying just to get something out of it, or hesitating to pray because you think there is nothing in it for you, but some people do think that way. We think we are sacrificing for the Lord by praying, but we are the biggest benefactors of all. We can be in a group praying for other people and nothing for ourselves, and we will walk away fully blessed by God. Not only are our prayers accomplishing much for others, but for ourselves as well—more than we even realize.

Engage Because You Serve God

God does not want our commitment to Him to be intimidating or overwhelming. He wants us to simply hear His call and answer it. It's about serving Him. It's not about us praying the perfect prayer. It's our perfect God answering the prayers we offer up to Him. It's not what we say that changes things; it's the power of God that attends our words. "The kingdom of God is *not in word but in power*" (1 Corinthians 4:20). Even though we are weak, we can be instruments of God's power. In fact, *because* we are weak we can be used mightily by God as an instrument of His power. "We have this treasure in earthen vessels, that *the excellence of the power may be of God and not of us*" (2 Corinthians 4:7).

We serve God by continuing to pray. He doesn't want us to pray once, and then if the prayer isn't answered to our liking we give up and say, "My prayers are not working." He wants us to stand strong and *keep praying*. He wants us to "be steadfast, immovable, *always abounding in the work of the Lord,* knowing that your labor is not in vain in the Lord" (1 Corinthians 15:58). That's why we can't sit in judgment on how God asks us to pray, or how we feel led by His Spirit to pray, or how He answers our prayer, or if we see results right away, or how we feel after we've prayed. We have to just pray without judgment.

God doesn't want us to stop praying when we go through tough times as if suddenly we are not qualified. Remember it is by *His* Spirit. By *His* strength and not our own. It is *His* armor protecting us, not ours. "We are hard-pressed on every side, yet not crushed; we are perplexed, but not in despair; persecuted, but not forsaken; struck down, but not destroyed—always carrying about in the body the dying of the Lord Jesus, that the life of Jesus also may be manifested in our body" (2 Corinthians 4:8-10). When we pray, God's power can be seen in us, even in our most difficult times. God wants us to be able to say as Paul said, "If we live, we live to the Lord; and if we die, we die to the Lord. Therefore, whether we live or die, we are the Lord's" (Romans 14:8). No matter what happens, we serve God because we are His.

When you pray as a prayer warrior, you are serving God directly and intimately. When you are praying for others, you are fulfilling God's will for them. When you advance the kingdom of God in prayer, you are forcing back the works of darkness. You are causing chains to break, allowing captives of the enemy to go free and bringing restoration where there has been none. You are causing healing and wholeness to take root where there has been sickness, brokenness, and suffering. You are bringing comfort where there has been despair. You are instilling hope where there has been hopelessness. You are revealing Jesus to those who have been transfixed by the trappings of false gods and idols. You are bringing the love of God where people don't even know it exists.

Don't think of being a prayer warrior as anything less than serving God because you love Him.

Whenever you pray for your own needs and the things heaviest on your heart, ask God to show you what else He wants you to pray for right then. God will show you by bringing a person, a people group, or a situation to your mind. He will reveal to you His heart for a person or situation. The Holy Spirit in you will help you to pray, and you will feel a passion about it—even moved to tears if it involves the suffering of others. You may be sensing the grief the Lord has over the situation, or you may be actually feeling that person's pain. You will know when God is *calling* you to pray for something or someone in a profound way because of that passion you feel while you are praying.

Just this morning as I sat down to write this, a picture of a young man who was severely injured in an accident and the grief of his mother came to mind, and I knew God was calling me to pray for them. I have been praying for them for many years, as have countless others, and we have seen miracles as this young man's life was not only saved but is being mended step by step. His recovery so far is a result of the prayers of many prayer warriors who heard the call of God to pray for miracle after miracle, and who won't stop responding to that call.

There is still a long way to go in this man's recovery, so I prayed for his specific needs of which I already knew. I prayed for the strength and comfort of his mother who has hardly left his side in all these years. I prayed for the other members of her family who have suffered terribly too. And as I was praying, God showed me specifics I had not thought of, and I prayed about those. He let me feel some of the grief his mother has carried and I wept, praying that my prayers would help lift that grief from her heart. I prayed for all the miracles they still need to see come to pass. And I prayed they would feel the assurance of those miracles ahead and that their hearts would have renewed hope.

God is calling you to hear His call to pray for someone right now. Ask Him who it is. When He brings someone to mind, ask the Holy Spirit to lead you as to how to pray. After you pray, don't question whether God has heard you or what He is doing about it. Just remember that there are two main truths about praying as a prayer warrior:

1. God hears your prayers.
2. God is answering in His way and His time.

You will never know all the good you have done with your prayers or what has been accomplished through them, but God does. If, for example, you pray as I have for a young girl enslaved in sex trafficking, you have no idea how your prayer might affect her situation. She may be able to escape or be rescued because of your prayers. If you are concerned that more people need to be praying with you about something, ask God to awaken the hearts of other prayer warriors to hear the call to pray for that situation too. It is His will to do that. But even if no one else is praying for that specific thing at that moment, the Holy Spirit is with you—*in* you—helping *you* to pray.

God sees your heart that you are willing to pray. He is not judging your prayers. He is pleased that you have the heart of a prayer warrior. The Bible says about giving that "there is first a willing mind" (2 Corinthians 8:12). You *have* a willing mind or you would not have come this far in the book. You have the desire to give of yourself to God by praying for others. The Bible says, "He who sows sparingly will also reap sparingly, and *he who sows bountifully will also reap bountifully*. So let each one give as he purposes in his heart, not grudgingly or of necessity; for God loves a cheerful giver" (2 Corinthians 9:6-7). You will reap great blessings because you love God and desire to serve Him with a joyful heart.

Engage Because You Know the Time Is Short

Evil is escalating and growing more intense. The stakes are getting higher. We can't just say, "Well, if it is going to happen, let it happen." Things can get far worse than they need to for a lot of people—especially believers in the Lord. We must pray for them to be protected. We must pray for people who have not hardened their hearts against the Lord to open up to Him as their Savior.

The time is short and we need to put on the armor of light. "The night is far spent, the day is at hand. Therefore let us cast off the works of darkness, and *let us put on the armor of light*" (Romans 13:12). "The armor of light" is the armor of God. It is His covering over us and His light within us. We must choose to put on all that Jesus is and has done for us in order to save, cover, and protect ourselves and others from evil. "Put on the Lord Jesus Christ, and make no provision for the flesh, to fulfill its lusts" (Romans 13:14).

If we don't understand this spiritual war, then our battle is always against people and groups. We end up struggling with humans instead of the evil powers who are controlling them. We get sidetracked in a battle of the flesh with people instead of battling with our spiritual weapons against the invisible works of darkness. We are called to pray in order to push back the darkness and advance the will of God on earth.

We have a spiritual enemy, not a flesh and blood enemy. We war against spiritual forces and powers who rule the darkness of this world and also wicked spirits in spiritual places over our cities and towns. It is important that we always keep in mind who our true enemy is. Otherwise, we are battling people in another political party. People of another race or social level. Or the boss at work. Or the unpleasant neighbor next door. Or the coworker from hell whom you have to deal with every day. If we start fighting with them, it not only exhausts us but doesn't accomplish anything. If we are battling people instead of the forces of darkness, then we are only defeating ourselves.

Engage Because You Are Engaged

When a woman is invited to go out to dinner with a man, but she has already promised to marry *another man*, she simply responds to the invitation by saying, "I am engaged." That's all she needs to say because that says it all. She is committed to someone, and she is not interested in anyone else.

When you are engaged with the Lord, you have promised to love and serve only Him. When other things cry out for your time and attention, there comes a point when you have to respond by saying, "I'm engaged. Engaged with my Lord. And I want to spend time with *Him*."

Being fully engaged with the Lord changes your life in the best possible ways. And it makes it easier to engage in the war against Him. That's why prayer warriors wholeheartedly engage in the spiritual war and pray with a sense of purpose—because they are first engaged with the Lord by loving and worshipping only Him. Their closeness to Him gives them heightened awareness of His heart on all matters and makes them sensitive to His will. They are so grateful for all He has done that they do not hesitate to go to battle for Him.

Know that we are not in danger by engaging in the war; we are in danger by not engaging in the war.

The way to engage with the Lord is to meet Him every morning and tell Him you love Him and worship Him and want to serve Him in any way He desires. The way you engage in the war is to present yourself to the Lord as His devoted prayer warrior who is listening for His every direction and is "*praying always with all prayer and supplication in the Spirit, being watchful to this end with all perseverance and supplication for all the saints*" (Ephesians 6:18).

Jesus said you can pray alone—just you and Him in private devotion. Or you can pray with another person—a *prayer partner*. Jesus said, "If two of you agree on earth concerning anything that they ask, it will be done for them by My Father in heaven" (Matthew 18:19). Or you can pray with two or more people—a *prayer group*. Jesus said, "Where two or three are gathered together in My name, I am there in the midst of them" (Matthew 18:20). No other grounds are needed for praying with other people. The unity of believers praying together has power because of the presence of Jesus and the assurance of answered prayer.

When you pray with someone else, the Holy Spirit in you is connected with the Holy Spirit in them and your prayers are powerful because of it.

However, if you pray with others, make sure you do not neglect your time alone with the Lord. If you are first engaged with Him, you will have a deep connection to Him that is like no other. And when distractions come to draw you away from your time with Him, you will miss Him too much to be away long.

As for me, I'm engaged. Are you engaged? Let's get engaged with God so we can be engaged in the war against us all. The enemy knows his time is short, and he is giving it everything he has. Shouldn't we give it all we have as well?

PRAYER FOR THE PRAYER WARRIOR

LORD, help me to engage with You in prayer every day in a powerful and effective way. I want to see Your will done on the earth, so I choose to engage in this war against our enemy. I commit to hear Your call to pray for people and situations as You lead me.

Thank You that You have given me protective armor, powerful weapons, and the promise that You are always with me. Help me to "cast off the works of darkness" and "put on the armor of light" (Romans 13:12). I know time is growing short because the enemy knows he has only a short time left to accomplish his evil plans. I know that as the time gets closer to Your return, the enemy wants as many hearts and minds sold out to him as he can get. Help me to always keep that in mind so that no matter what is happening in me, around me, or in the world, I am praying for Your will to be done.

I am grateful to be part of Your great army of prayer warriors who have heard Your call to pray and are listening every day for Your instructions. I am excited to see what all You will do through our prayers. Help me to not sit in judgment on my prayers or Your answers. I commit to simply praying and leaving the answer in Your hands to accomplish in Your way, in Your time, and according to Your will. I want to serve You and *Your* plans because I love You and am grateful to You for all You've done for me and will do in the future.

Help me to stand strong in the simplicity that is in Christ. Teach me to identify true spiritual power and not feigned spirituality. Help me to not succumb to spiritual or theological quarreling with people because Your Word says it is never productive. Enable me to always hear Your call to pray. Give me Your heart for people and the struggles they are in. Help me to pray right on target every time. I engage in the spiritual war because I am engaged completely with You and want to serve You well.

In Jesus' name I pray.

> *Rejoice, O heavens, and you who dwell in them!*
> *Woe to the inhabitants of the earth and the sea!*
> *For the devil has come down to you,*
> *having great wrath,*
> *because he knows that he has a short time.*
>
> REVELATION 12:12

9

IDENTIFY THE
IMMEDIATE BATTLEFIELD

God has given us His kingdom here on earth, but if we don't move into it the way He asks us to, we can get too close to the edge and fall into enemy territory. God doesn't want that for us, and neither do we. Jesus said, "Do not fear, little flock, for it is your Father's good pleasure to give you the kingdom" (Luke 12:32). God wants us to enjoy the full benefits of His kingdom not only in eternity, but on earth as well. The eternity part is a sure thing. Here on earth we must do *our* part to see that the kingdom of God advances—both *in us* and *in the world around us*. As prayer warriors, we do that in prayer.

The most dangerous place you can be in this war is on the sidelines of God's kingdom. *Barely in* is way too close to enemy territory. *Barely in* doesn't mean barely saved. If you have received Jesus you are saved. But if you never move in His Word and obedience to His ways, you will not be enjoying all the benefits that kingdom living affords. God has more for you than that. The outer edge of God's kingdom is where you will be shot at most. You may experience one attack after another and blame God for it instead of identifying the enemy and the battlefield.

God has given the responsibility for the advancement of His kingdom on earth to us—His children. We are partners in the family business. Jesus said, "From the days of John the Baptist until now the kingdom of heaven suffers violence, and the violent take it by force" (Matthew 11:12). God *gives* us the kingdom, but we still have to *take* it. If you give someone a gift and they don't *take* it, then they don't possess it. We have to take God's kingdom in order to possess the fullness of it. We have to take it into our own lives, and we take it to places where it is not. That means we have to get dangerous in prayer—dangerous to the enemy, that is. We have to break through every barrier the enemy erects to keep us from becoming all God created us to be and doing what God calls us to do in order to advance His kingdom on earth.

In order to do that, it is important to not only know exactly who our enemy is, but to also be able to clearly identify the battlefield. That is, where the true battle is at the moment. Of course, the battlefield is always wherever you are praying. That's because prayer is the battle, and *you* choose the time and place. But there are specific battlefields beyond that where the enemy attacks. It is wherever he thinks he can insert himself like a wedge into your life or the lives of others.

A good soldier always knows the layout of the battlefield as much as he possibly can, and we must know that too. The battlefield is where the enemy brings the battle to you. Some of the battlefields the enemy likes to attack you on are your relationships, work, finances, family, and health. For the purpose of illustrating the power of God moving in response to the prayers of a prayer warrior, I want to give you three examples of the enemy's battlefields. They are the battlefield for your mind, the battlefield for your children's lives, and the battlefield for your marriage. These are all popular with the enemy as his favorite areas to attack our lives and create havoc. You don't have to have been attacked in these areas in order to learn from the examples, because they will help you see how the prayers of prayer warriors can defeat the enemy on *any* battlefield.

The Battlefield in the Fight for Your Clarity of Mind

There is a major war zone that is not in the government, or in crime-infested neighborhoods, or in a computer hacker's mind, or in the realm of a human trafficker, drug dealer, child molester, or rapist. It is in the invisible realm that is every bit as real as the physical. It is the battlefield of our mind.

Again, I must repeat this here because it is too important not to. If you have received Jesus as your Savior, you have the Holy Spirit of God in you. He is the seal that you are owned by God and you belong to Him. The enemy cannot have control of your mind, but he can still lie to you and wage a battle there. And then it becomes your own personal battlefield.

In our mind we express our will and make decisions and choices that affect our lives and the lives of others. It is one of the enemy's favorite places because he can use his lies to greatest advantage.

The enemy uses our own feelings of guilt, condemnation, fear, anxiety, worthlessness, hopelessness, self-hatred, and other negative emotions against us. These thoughts and feelings are in us because of what has happened to us in our past, even as recently as yesterday. Somewhere along the line we bought into the lies of the enemy. And because we are not aware of what God's Word clearly says about us—or we don't fully believe it—we don't discern what the enemy is doing. When we know the truth, we can put on the whole armor of God and use God's Word as not only our shield of faith to combat those lies, but also as our greatest weapon against the purveyor of them.

I had a battle going on in my mind from the time I was a young girl. I was raised by a mentally ill mother. She was verbally and physically abusive, but I believe her locking me in the closet much of my early childhood did the most damage. She frequently told me I was worthless and would never amount to anything. She said I didn't deserve to have anything, especially happiness or success in life. As a result of all that, I grew up with every negative emotion anyone can have. I constantly heard those lies recited over and over in my mind. I desperately searched for a way out of my misery and couldn't find one—except for suicide. In my late twenties, as I was planning to take my life once I collected enough sleeping pills, a friend I worked with saw I was not doing well and took me to meet her pastor, who led me to the Lord.

When I received Jesus, the most beautiful life-giving light came into the darkness where I had been living all my life. The more I learned the truth about Him and what He had done for me, the more I recognized the battle in my mind and how I needed to be free of it. People prayed for me to be set free of those negative thought patterns, and one by one they disappeared and I was totally liberated.

Today I know I never have to be tormented by negative, self-destructive thoughts again. I have been set free of them because of prayer warriors praying for me and because I understand the Word of God regarding these things. No one else who has received the Lord and has the Holy Spirit living in them has to put up with this battle in their mind either.

When we have a battle going on in our mind between *our* will and *God's*, between *good* and *evil*, between *truth* and *lies*, the Word of God will clarify our thoughts. The enemy will always try to get you to question God's Word just as he did with Eve. She did not stand strong in what she knew God had said. The enemy tried to tempt Jesus in the wilderness, but He stood strong by battling the enemy with the Word of God.

You must recognize when the enemy is using your mind as a battlefield. If you think the battlefield is with your mean coworker, or an abusive family member, or a person at school who insulted you, you will not see how the enemy is trying to stir up pain and turmoil and strife in your mind and emotions. You must take the battlefield away from the enemy and bring it into your prayer closet.

If you are living with depression, anger, the inability to forgive, severe loneliness, doubt, fear, anxiety, hopelessness, feelings of futility, feeling unloved, or as if it is you against everyone else, know that these negative thoughts are the enemy's favorite tactic against you. He is taking his war to your most vulnerable place. He can probably get us there easier than anyplace else because we are quick to think that this misery is just the way we are. Or that we *deserve* to feel this way.

When the battlefield is your mind, you will experience tormenting, confusing, or negative thoughts; irrational fears or extreme doubt; anger; or other destructive emotions. But the Bible says we are to deliberately think about opposite things: Paul said, "Whatever things are *true*, whatever things are *noble*, whatever things are *just*, whatever things are *pure*, whatever things are *lovely*, whatever things are of *good report*, if there is any *virtue* and if there is anything *praiseworthy*—meditate on these things" (Philippians 4:8). Dwelling on these things that are true will help you to identify the thoughts that are not.

We cannot afford to ignore this battlefront. In fact, you should secure this front first before going on to others so you will not be weakened. You don't need to be fighting the battle on two fronts. It's not that you can't do that. You *can* fight a personal battle and do warfare for others at the same time. But dealing with the personal first makes you stronger in all areas.

The Battlefield in the Fight for Your Children's Lives

The enemy always wants your children, and he will try to destroy them or win them in whatever way he can. That's why you should daily ask God to show you if the enemy is attacking one of your children. If, for example, your child has gotten in with the wrong people, or has developed bad habits, or seems to be attracted to the wrong things, you can be sure the enemy is setting a trap for that child. Recognize that the battlefield is not with your child; it is with the enemy. You must stand your ground in prayer on that battlefield where your child has been attacked and take your child back from the enemy's clutches. Now don't freak out and get scared that you have to talk to the enemy—I know how some of you are. You don't have to. But you must take dominion over the forces of darkness attempting to work in that child's life. And that happens in prayer.

Don't cower in fear before any enemy threat on your child. Stand on God's Word and claim your child for God's kingdom. No matter how many times you have done it before, do it again. Declare the Word of God. Recall the day you dedicated that child to the Lord. If you haven't done that, do it now. If the enemy has an entrance into your life because of sin, confess it and get it straight with God. Don't give the enemy power because of your own unconfessed sin. Yes, your sins can come down on your child. The sins of the fathers are visited upon the children to the third and fourth generation unless they are broken by you or by the child, or by someone who is strong in faith and the Word of God. We have seen too many instances of where a parent's sinful choices have left a child uncovered and trouble finds them.

If your child is young, he does not know how to do battle for himself against the enemy. But *you do*. So do it. Don't back down. Your child is the Lord's. Claim him for God's kingdom. Even if you have to do that every day until that child is free, keep on doing it.

My husband and I battled for our children's lives, especially when they were teenagers. I asked God every day to reveal anything happening in their lives that I needed to see. And God would show me what was going on. When my husband and I had to confront them on anything, we prayed together *first* because this battle had to be won in the spirit realm before it could ever be won in their lives. The enemy had to be exposed and his influence broken. My children told me many times that they hated the fact they could never get away with anything. Later, when they were adults, they thanked us for that.

Sometimes the problems were because of choices they were

making, such as listening to ungodly music. They would bring it into the house, and we would throw it away. They would put up posters glorifying ungodly music groups, and we would tear them down. Eventually they realized it just wasn't worth it, so they stopped doing it. We recognized that this battlefield was where the enemy was trying to gain the minds and allegiances of our son and daughter. Nearly every parent faces this battle in this time and culture. We battled the enemy in spiritual warfare and refused to battle with our children. We simply informed them that they were not going to bring detestable things into our house and what the consequences would be if they did. I am not saying the battle in prayer wasn't fierce and long. It was! But we did not give in. And those strongholds were eventually broken.

There were other battles when the enemy was trying to trap them or destroy them. One such incident I have never told publicly before, but a couple of close friends have known about it. It happened when my daughter was 18. She had an entry-level job that required her to work three evenings a week. I was concerned about that because it meant that after work she had to walk to her car in a dimly lit parking lot at night. Even though others were leaving at the same time, I knew she was way too trusting of people—especially those she *thought* she knew but didn't. I prayed for her all the time, but certainly on those evenings when she was working. I could never really sleep or rest easy until she was back home.

While I didn't like that my young daughter was out on her own late at night, I knew she needed to learn the value of a dollar, and how hard people needed to work, and how responsible they had to be. It didn't take her long to see that.

She always called me after work when she got in her car to tell me she was on her way. One particular night she called me and said, "Mom, I am on my way home," the way she always did, but there was something about that call that bothered me. I heard something different in her voice, and I knew the Holy Spirit was prompting me to pray. So after we hung up I started to pray for her. I knew I was doing warfare and the battlefield was her life because I was drawn to intercede for her beyond what I usually did. I grew especially concerned when she wasn't home within twenty minutes as she normally would have been. I prayed over and over that no weapon formed against her would prosper. I prayed for God's protection. I didn't call her back because I didn't like her driving while talking on a cell phone. I felt that wasn't safe.

When she finally came home about fifteen minutes later than usual, I went to meet her to see if everything was okay. She said she was very glad to be home and that it had been an exhausting night, and then she headed quickly up to bed. I thought it was unusual that she didn't stay in the kitchen to grab something to eat and talk a little, but I could see she was exhausted.

It was some time later before she told me what actually happened that night. She said she delayed in telling me because she knew I would not be pleased that she had violated one of our rules.

She worked at a place that gave music lessons, and she was one of the instructors. A young man came in three nights a week, so she had seen him nearly every night she worked there. Over the preceding months they had talked a little every time. He was not one of her clients and their conversations were brief, but he was always quite pleasant to talk to and seemed very nice and polite. At the end of that one evening when all the classes were over, he asked her to go have coffee with him to continue a conversation they had begun earlier. Not being discerning about the true nature of people, she said yes. I had told her countless times to never go anywhere with someone you don't know well. She thought because she had frequently seen him at the place where she worked that she knew him well enough to go out in public for thirty minutes.

Another thing I had instructed her on specifically—and she held to that—was to never get into a car with someone else driving, especially a man. I told her, "*You* always drive. *You* be in control of the car. Even if the person does not intend to do wrong, you don't know how safe a driver that person is." The man suggested right away that she drive and she took that as a good sign. He said he would direct her to their destination because she wasn't familiar with the area. She had only driven to her workplace and nowhere else.

He got into the car with her and told her which way to turn out of the parking lot and what way to turn on the main road. After a few more turns, he told her to turn right onto a narrow road that went winding up a mountain slope thick with trees on either side. She wanted to turn around immediately, but the overgrowth was so lush on both sides of the road that there was nowhere to turn around. And it was pitch black in there, so backing up would have been impossible. She was trapped in her car on a narrow single-lane road with trees so close she couldn't have even opened her car door. She didn't want to go any farther but saw no alternative.

She became frightened and began to cry. He had no response. She felt that her life was in danger and this was it for her. She started desperately praying out loud, "Jesus, help me! Jesus, save me!" over and over. The man who seemed friendly to her at work suddenly changed and became cold and unfeeling and had no sympathy whatsoever for her crying. He didn't ask why she was crying. He knew.

Even her crying out for Jesus to rescue her didn't faze this man. He became an entirely different person, clearly intent on doing something despite her pleas. He obviously had another plan in mind. And my daughter knew she might not get out of this situation alive. She was beside herself with fear.

The road led nowhere but to a tiny clearing. There was nothing and no one up there, and it was completely dark except for the car's headlights. She knew she was trapped and she had the most horrific, sickening feeling as to what was about to happen. She knew she could be raped and killed up there and her body disposed of in the woods and never found. By that time she was sobbing convulsively, but the man was still without any feeling whatsoever.

He told her to stop there and get out of the car. He got out of the car immediately, leaving his car door open so she couldn't lock the doors and escape. There was still not enough room to turn around and go back down the mountain.

It was so dark there that when the man had only taken two steps away from the car she could no longer see him. Again he said sternly, "Get out of the car!"

She said, "Okay, I'm coming," trying to buy time, at which point she grabbed her phone and called me. She said she made herself talk as normally as possible so as not to upset him. That's when she told me she was on her way home so he would know someone was expecting her.

At that point she wasn't sure where he was because she couldn't see him. She was afraid he would appear on her side of the car. She locked her door and decided there was no way she would leave that car and let him take her into the woods. He would have to kill her in the car. As she was contemplating how she could fight against him, the man suddenly came running out of the woods in terror and jumped back into the car. He slammed the door and yelled, "Go! Go! Go! There is something horrible in the woods!" He was extremely frightened and desperate.

She did what he asked.

He directed her down the other side of the mountain because it was impossible to go back down the way they had come up. But this side of the mountain road was extremely winding and had a drop-off down the mountain on the driver's side. She could see that much.

The man kept yelling, "Faster! Go faster!" But she felt she was already going too fast for that treacherous road.

He was obviously petrified and kept saying "There is something horrible out there."

"What did you see?" she asked.

"I don't know…it was horrible…I can't…it's terrifying…there is something horrible out there." He was genuinely distraught.

"What did you see?" she asked again. But he could not even put three words together to describe it.

He didn't say one more word to her all the way back to his car, where she dropped him off. He was still visibly shaken when he got out of her car and rushed to his. She left for home immediately. She never saw him again. And shortly after that she quit her job.

Later she wondered, *How could he see anything in that pitch-black night? If it was a person or an animal, he could have described that. If it was an inanimate object, he could have said that.* She told me that whatever it was in the forest, it gave her peace. She knew it was from the Lord.

After she told me her story I described to her how I was led to pray for her that night. I told her how I could not let go of the uneasy feeling I had, so I prayed for her protection and that no weapon formed against her would prosper, and no plan of the enemy would succeed in her life. I prayed specifically, over and over, that the Lord would surround her with angels. At that moment we both came to the exact same conclusion—that whatever that man saw that suddenly weakened him with fright was *sent by God*. Something indescribable to an unbeliever was there in that forest. And God sent whatever it was. We believe he saw giant warrior angels with swords drawn, or possibly the angel of the Lord. He did not just *sense* their frightening presence because he *saw* something.

So often in the Bible when an angel sent by God appears to someone, the first thing he said to them was, "Do not be afraid." People were afraid even when the angel was coming with good news for them. These angels are larger than life and terrifying to behold. Imagine how menacing an angel like that with a sword drawn coming in a threatening way to an unbeliever who is about to do something evil against a child of God would be. The Bible says, "He shall give His angels charge over you, to keep you in all your ways. In their hands they shall bear you up, lest you dash your foot against a stone" (Psalm 91:11-12). Imagine how much more so when two prayer warriors are crying desperately for rescue out of the jaws of death.

The angel of the Lord is mentioned many times in the Bible. "The LORD opened Balaam's eyes, and he saw the Angel of the LORD standing in the way with His drawn sword in His hand; and he bowed his head and fell flat on his face" (Numbers 22:31). It also says, "The angel of the LORD encamps all around those who fear Him and delivers them" (Psalm 34:7).

That incident changed my daughter's life. She was always a strong person of prayer, but she saw the power of God manifested in an unforgettable way on her behalf in response to prayer. She has never been the same since. While she is not so trusting of others, she is very trusting of God's hand of protection in her life.

This is what being a prayer warrior is all about. It's about consistent praying and making those prayer deposits in that heavenly bank until one day you need a major withdrawal. I believe that those years my husband and I prayed for our daughter's safety were accumulative. And they needed to be. They were lifesaving against the plans of the enemy.

Our prayers have power. Don't ever believe otherwise. The more you pray, the more power they will have, and the more answers to prayer you will see. We went to battle in prayer and the enemy was defeated. Praise be to God, our prayers added up to a miracle.

The Battlefield in the Fight for Your Marriage

The enemy attacks wherever he thinks he can. That is, any place he sees vulnerability. One of those areas is marriage. He doesn't like marriage because it is something God established, and it is through marriage that offspring are born and raised and God is glorified in the family. And the enemy does not want God to be glorified because he is obsessed with pursuing his own glory.

The enemy will attack on the battlefield of your marriage whenever he can. If there is selfishness on the part of either a husband or wife, the enemy can work in the midst of that weakness. His favorite ploy is stirring up strife between a husband and wife so that they hurt each other with their harsh words and actions and never think to blame the enemy for inciting it. They blame each other instead.

The person we love the most can also hurt us the most, especially in a marriage. But we must not react to them as if *they* are the enemy. We must go instead to God in prayer and ask Him to show us the truth about what is happening. Don't be pulled into a battle with your spouse. Be pulled close to God and proclaim His truth against the enemy.

My marriage had problems right from the beginning because I came into it with a lot of hurt and negative thoughts about myself that had been instilled in me from childhood. My husband came into the marriage with a lot of anger because of certain hurtful experiences in his past as well. His anger directed at me caused me to hurt even more, and my withdrawal from him made him ever angrier. The strife between us became unbearable.

When we were finally able to see that the battlefield the enemy had chosen for us was our marriage, then we began making progress. We had to recognize where the turmoil was coming from and go to battle against it in prayer. I have made a much longer story very short and simple here in order to make the point, but in case you are interested, I have written the full story in my book *The Power of a Praying® Wife*.

There are countless people all over the world who are prayer warriors for their marriage. I don't even see how you can keep a marriage together without vigilant prayer. Even if you are the only one praying, you can see a miracle. That is, unless your mate is so strong willed that he or she refuses to hear from God. In that case, release him or her into God's hands. He has a way of speaking to our heart the way nothing else can.

Whenever you are being attacked, determine where the battlefield is that the enemy has brought you to. It is important to have clarity on exactly what the boundaries are of the battle you are fighting. Is it personal—in your mind, emotions, body, soul, or heart? In your children? In your marriage? In your work? In your health? Is it on behalf of other people? Which people and where? Is it in a relationship? With a neighbor? A coworker? Your church? Where? What? Be as specific as possible so you can be clear on where the enemy has taken the battle. Wherever it is, take the battlefield back to where *you* choose—your own prayer closet.

Prayer for the Prayer Warrior

LORD, I know the battlefield is wherever I am praying because prayer *is* the battle. But when the enemy brings the battle to me, help me to discern exactly what that battlefield is. Enable me to see the truth about what I am fighting against. Help me to be so clear about this that I know exactly how to pray. Enable me to understand what You are calling me to pray for and how. Teach me to recognize the plans of the enemy and take dominion over his tactics in prayer.

Whenever I hear a prompting from Your Spirit, keep me from ignoring it. When You are telling me to pray about a person or situation, enable me to hear from You specifically and not be too tired or too preoccupied to pray. Teach me to respond immediately. I know that the "weapons of our warfare are not carnal but mighty in God for pulling down strongholds" (2 Corinthians 10:4). Teach me to pull down every stronghold the enemy is trying to erect in my life and the lives of others whom You put on my heart. Help me to refute every argument or high thing that exalts itself against You, Your ways, and Your will.

Enable me to always see clearly what the enemy is doing so I can identify the battlefield where he is waging war against me. Help me to clearly see when the enemy of my soul is attacking my mind with negativity. Teach me to immediately bring my thoughts and feelings under Your control and into obedience to Your ways (2 Corinthians 10:5). Help me to bring every thought captive under Your Lordship. I know that my weapons are spiritual, and I am empowered by

You to use them on any battlefield that presents itself to me. Thank You that Your angel encamps around me and delivers me and those for whom I pray (Psalm 34:7). Thank You that You give Your angels charge over me and my family to keep us safe and bear us up when we stumble (Psalm 91:11-12).

In Jesus' name I pray.

Though we walk in the flesh,
we do not war according to the flesh.
For the weapons of our warfare are not carnal
but mighty in God
for pulling down strongholds,
casting down arguments
and every high thing that exalts itself
against the knowledge of God,
bringing every thought into captivity
to the obedience of Christ.

2 CORINTHIANS 10:3-5

10

FOLLOW HIS ORDERS TO RESIST THE ENEMY

How do we get the enemy to stop harassing us? God's Word says, "Resist the devil and he will flee from you" (James 4:7). But how do we resist?

The three words before those say, "*Submit to God.*"

"Submit" is a military term, and it means to obey or to be subordinate to a commander. You hear about soldiers getting charged with insubordination. That means they did not obey their commanding officer. We don't ever want to be charged with insubordination by God. We want to submit to Him the way a soldier *submits* to his commander. Without question.

When James was talking to the people he was writing to about their sins, he told them that their friendship with the world had made them enemies of God. They were asking for things from God but not receiving them because they asked with entirely selfish motives (James 4:1-5). God wanted to be first in their hearts.

God wants to be first in our hearts too. When we do things that separate us from Him in any way, our prayers don't get answered.

What separates us from God? *Sin* does. *Worldliness* does. *Pride* does (James 4:6). These three accompany each other. But what can put a stop to all that in our lives?

Humility can.

Resist the Enemy by Rejecting Pride

The cure for pride, worldliness, and sin is humility. That is the cure for many things. Humility comes by totally submitting ourselves to God.

Submitting to God means humbling ourselves before Him and declaring our utter dependence upon Him. It means repenting of all pride.

The enemy knows our weaknesses. That's why our every weakness must be submitted to God so His Spirit can enable us to be strong in those areas. Do you ever wonder why we have seen too many Christian leaders fall into immorality? It's because they had areas in their lives that were not submitted to God, and the enemy could plant a lure in those places. The enemy—and the person the enemy used—could first of all appeal to their pride. Someone flattered them and they were puffed up by it. Pride is blinding! Their pride caused them to think they were above the laws of God—and sometimes above the laws of men. When pride finds a home in anyone, that person becomes aligned with the enemy—they have pride in common, after all—and he will lead them where God never intended for them to go.

Any unsubmitted area in us is dangerous. Wherever we don't submit to God in our lives is an automatic invitation to the enemy. That's why the first step to resisting the enemy is to submit to God in every way.

We have to be completely grounded in the things of God. We have to live on such a solid foundation that our life is not shaken when the enemy comes to trap us in our own pride. When we resist the devil by resisting pride, the enemy sees he is wasting his time on us and flees to someone more receptive to his enticements.

It doesn't matter how powerfully the enemy comes against us. If we set ourselves to resist him—and this happens in our heart the moment we make that decision—the enemy cannot prevail against us.

But we have to first submit to God.

Only when we submit to God first can we successfully resist the devil. Trying to resist without first submitting to God is a losing battle. We can't begin to resist him on our own without the power of God in us. Only then can we truly draw near to God, cleanse our hands, purify our hearts, grieve over our sins, be mournful of our failures, cry out to God for forgiveness by confessing and repenting, and humble ourselves before the Lord. When the Lord sees us bowing in humility before Him, He lifts us up.

Jesus said, "*Everyone who exalts himself will be humbled, and he who humbles himself will be exalted*" (Luke 18:14). When we humble ourselves before Him, He extends His *grace* to us. And we can't resist the enemy successfully without God's grace. God has set Himself to bring down the prideful. And He will exalt the humble. His Word says, "*Humble yourselves under the mighty hand of God, that He may exalt you in due time*, casting all your care upon Him, for He cares for you" (1 Peter 5:6-7).

Submit to God by humbling yourself before Him, and He will lift you up.

When we resist pride, we are resisting the enemy. When we draw close to God, He responds in kind. "Draw near to God and He will draw near to you. Cleanse your hands, you sinners; and purify your hearts, you double-minded" (James 4:8). Being double-minded means wavering back and forth with one foot in the world and one in God's kingdom. We can never receive all God has for us when we do that. We must cleanse our desires so completely that we are grieved over any pride, sin, or worldliness we see in ourselves. Our full recognition of that will cause us to mourn (James 4:9). And that is a good thing.

The proud resist God, but God resists the proud (James 4:6).

The last thing we need is to have God resist us.

Wars and fighting come basically from rebellion against God (James 4:1-2). That happens when we want what *we* want and don't care what *God* wants. All sin is lawlessness. All lawlessness is *rebellion against God. The root of rebellion against God is pride.* Pride causes people to go to war with God by being friends with God's enemy.

Abraham chose to be a friend of God. "Abraham believed God, and it was accounted to him for righteousness. And he was called the *friend of God*" (James 2:23). Abraham's nephew, Lot, chose to be a friend of the world. As a result, Abraham was blessed by God, and Lot ended up losing everything. We must choose to be *God's* friend and never side with the enemy. That means caring more about what *God* thinks of us than what anyone else thinks.

God revives us when we are humble. "For thus says the high and lofty One who inhabits eternity, whose name is Holy: '*I dwell in the high and holy place, with him who has a contrite and humble spirit, to revive the spirit of the humble,* and to revive the heart of the contrite ones'" (Isaiah 57:15). God dwells with us when we are humble before Him.

God hears our prayers when we are humble. "LORD, *You have heard the desire of the humble;* You will prepare their heart; You will cause Your ear to hear" (Psalm 10:17). When we recognize our pride and respond to it with sorrow and repentance in our heart, we can be cleansed and renewed.

Don't let the enemy tell you that submitting to God will cause you to miss out on some great worldly thing. Actually, the opposite is true. Submitting to the enemy will limit all God has for you. Submitting to *God* brings blessings far beyond what you can imagine into your life. What you gain is so far superior to anything the world has to offer.

The enemy wants us to be separated from God, but he can only separate us if we listen to *him* instead of *God's truth.* When we submit to God and His ways, we will not align ourselves with evil. We all face the enemy's enticement to be prideful in one way or another in our lives. Prayer warriors are humble people. It is their nature to love God and care about others. They would suffer to think that they had grieved God and made the Holy Spirit yearn for them, like a parent grieves and yearns for a wayward son or daughter. But pride can creep into any one of us. We cannot ignore that possibility. That's why we must pray frequently that we will resist the enemy by staying humble before God. And that happens with every step of submission to God we take.

Resist the Enemy by Refusing Fear

You are made up of *"spirit, soul,* and *body"*—your soul is made up of your *mind* and *emotions*, and this includes your *will* (1 Thessalonians 5:23). God wants all of these aspects of you submitted to Him under His Lordship. If the enemy has influence in any of these areas of yourself, you will find fear creeping into your soul.

Fear increases in us when we have too much involvement with the world. If you suffer from fear, the enemy will seize the opportunity to feed it in you until you are emotionally paralyzed. That's one of the reasons so many people are on medication. Their problems have fear as their root—fear of failure, fear of not living up to some standard, fear of the future, fear of judgment, fear of criticism, fear of man, fear of everything. Out of curiosity, I looked through a book on fears and phobias and was shocked to find that they are as numerous as the stars. There is a phobia for everything on earth. And where do these countless fears come from? Not from God. Fear is the work of the enemy in our lives. We become afraid when we listen to the voice of the enemy and not the voice of God.

I am in no way critical of anyone who takes medicine. Not in the least. Take it when you need it. I have known people with different phobias, and these fears are very real to the person being tormented by them. I'm just saying God has freedom from fear. And His freedom is free.

Before I came to the Lord, I was tormented with various fears every day of my life. Mostly they were "what if" fears. "What if someone breaks in?" "What if I fail?" "What if they reject me?" "What if I am in an accident?" "What if I get a deadly disease?" I remember so well how awful it felt to be nearly paralyzed with fear. It was more than just fear; it was terror. It was a spirit of fear from the enemy.

Once I came to the Lord, my depression and anxiety were so severe that I sought Christian counseling from a gifted pastor's wife. She advised me to go on a three-day fast—and she fasted with me— and when it was over she and another pastor's wife prayed for me, and I was set free of all fear, depression, and anxiety. I felt all of that lift. They told me that, "*God has not given us a spirit of fear,* but of *power* and of *love* and of a *sound mind*" (2 Timothy 1:7). From that point on, I did not think about fear. It was gone, along with the depression and anxiety. It was miraculous. My life was changed from then on. I praised God for the power, love, and sound mind He had given me.

I feel I must say here that my fear, depression, and anxiety were caused by a deep wounding of my soul because of abuse I suffered in childhood. I had tried medicine, and it did nothing for me except make me feel more hopeless. It was the overwhelming love and power of God that took all that mental and emotional torment away, and I was never paralyzed by it again. I am not saying I was never depressed, anxious, or fearful from that moment on. Things happen in our lives that cause us to feel that way. But if I ever felt anything like that, I went directly to the Lord and to His Word and it would go away immediately. The enemy had no influence like that in my life from then on.

Some people experience fear, depression, and anxiety and *do* require medical help. And it is not because of anything terrible that happened in their past. There is just something their body needs. If you need medicine from a doctor and it is helping you, take it and thank God for that help. This is nothing to feel bad about in any way. Don't be discouraged about it. It doesn't disqualify you for anything in God's eyes. You have value and purpose like everyone else, so don't let the enemy lie to you and tell you any different. We all have things we struggle with. Just keep praying that your doctor and you have wisdom about what will help you most.

One common fear for many people is that our past will control our future. That is, we are destined to repeat the failures and devastation of our past. Nothing could be further from the truth. This is another lie of the enemy. The truth is, you are not your past. You are a new creation in Christ. This is not to say you should *ignore* the past. Acknowledge it for what it was. If it was terrible and damaging to you, if it was hurtful and you know it caused great scars in your mind and emotions, don't deny it. Bring it all to the Lord. God will redeem everything by bringing good out of it. It's one of the countless miracles He does.

Paul said that he lived "*forgetting those things which are behind* and *reaching forward to those things which are ahead,* I press toward the goal for the prize of the upward call of God in Christ Jesus" (Philippians 3:13-14). We must do the same. God will help you step out of your past and reach toward the future He has for you. And fear will not be part of that process.

Fear is one of the enemy's weapons against us. Refuse to buy into it. Know God's truth so well that you don't allow the world to control your thoughts or determine the level of your peace. Do not permit yourself to become drawn into the many conflicts around you so that you are brought down by them. Refuse to allow the media to fill you with fear as they try to direct your thoughts and manipulate your doubts. Don't tolerate outside influences in the world distracting you from what is happening in the spirit realm. Refuse to be overwhelmed because *God* is not overwhelmed. Resist all confusion. Thank God every day for the *sound mind of clarity* He has given you. There is only one purveyor of fear and confusion, and you know who that is.

Resist the Enemy by Praying for Miracles

When Peter was in prison, "constant prayer was offered to God for him by the church" (Acts 12:5). Many people were led by the Spirit to pray fervently for him.

While he was asleep in prison *and bound by two chains, between two soldiers,* and *with guards at the prison door, "an angel of the Lord stood by him* and a light shone in the prison; and he struck Peter on the side" and told him to get up, *and his chains fell off of him* (Acts 12:7). The angel instructed Peter to put on his sandals and follow him, and not only did they walk right past the soldiers and guards, but *the iron gate automatically opened for them.* When he came to the house where the people were still praying, they couldn't believe it was Peter at their door. It was an even greater miracle than they thought could happen.

The fervent, unceasing, Spirit-led prayers of believers brought Peter's miraculous deliverance out of the enemy's hands. *While they were praying, his chains fell off,* the guards were put to sleep, and the iron gates opened. You never know how your prayers may set a captive free.

God wants to do miracles through us, but too often we either don't pray for them, or don't believe they can happen, or when they *do* happen we have trouble believing it. The enemy not only does not want God's miracles to happen—because they are never to his advantage—but he will always try to steal away the miracle God has done by bringing doubt about it. Even when a miracle happens, the enemy will try to erase it. When Jesus raised Lazarus from the dead, the religious men who were working against Jesus tried to destroy the miracle by plotting to put Lazarus to death themselves (John 12:10). They did not want news of that miracle to spread. As the kingdom of God advances and miracles happen, the enemy will seek every opportunity to try to discredit each one.

When God delivered the Israelites out of slavery, they fled to the Red Sea, at which point they could go no farther. They saw the enormous army of Egyptians coming after them, and instead of being full of faith because of all the miracles they had just witnessed, they complained that they should have stayed in slavery in Egypt. They possibly didn't pray for another miracle because they couldn't even imagine one that would save them. Who could imagine the Red Sea parting to let them go across on dry land? But that's the point. Too often, just because we cannot imagine the miracle, we don't pray for it. We have to stop doing that. We must trust in our miracle-working God and pray for a miracle without feeling we have to tell Him how to do it.

Even after the Israelites were rescued by the parting of the Red Sea and the drowning of the Egyptian army, they did not trust God. They still wanted their old enslavement back because it was more familiar to them than their new freedom. Freedom was too much work. They didn't pray for miracles because their life without miracles in slavery in Egypt seemed easier.

The Bible says, "Be *sober*, be *vigilant*; because *your adversary the devil* walks about like a roaring lion, *seeking whom he may devour. Resist him, steadfast in the faith,* knowing that the same sufferings are experienced by your brotherhood in the world" (1 Peter 5:8-9). The enemy attacks and deceives believers all over the world every day, but we can resist his tactics, not only for ourselves, but for anyone anywhere. In Paul's first letter to Timothy, he instructed him to "wage the good warfare" (1 Timothy 1:18). His words speak to us that *we* can wage the good warfare as well because the Holy Spirit gives us the weapons and power we need to do it.

Our service to God as prayer warriors is not to be dreaded or avoided. It is to be *embraced*. We have Holy Spirit–ignited power and we must not allow the enemy to tell us any differently. We must follow God's orders to resist the enemy by praying for miracles until we sense the presence of the Lord with us either making them happen or releasing us from that specific prayer burden.

Pray that God will deliver us from unbelief and increase our faith to believe for miracles.

When God puts it on your heart to pray for something, don't doubt whether you can pray effectively or think that what you are praying for could not possibly happen. All prayer warriors must be convinced that God can work a miracle at any time, and that His power is not limited to what we *think* or *feel* He will do—or what someone of little faith decides He can't do. We are to just pray for a miracle. It's in God's hands from that point.

Resist the Enemy by Not Giving Up

Submitting to God means doing all He asks you to do. It means standing *up* for Him. Resisting the enemy means *not* doing anything he wants you to do. It means standing *against* him.

If you are listening to the enemy's lies, then you are not standing strong against him. He recognizes when your resolve is weak. He also knows when it is impenetrable and he is wasting his time with you. So he leaves, vowing to come back in one of your weak moments. But when you resolve to stay dependent on the Lord and *His* strength, then you are strong enough to avoid weak moments.

Jesus said that "men always ought to pray and not lose heart" (Luke 18:1).

Don't become discouraged and stop praying. The enemy wins that way. And don't worry about the hardships you go through. They do not disqualify you from being a powerful prayer warrior. "Our light affliction, which is but for a moment, is working for us a far more exceeding and eternal weight of glory, while *we do not look at the things which are seen, but at the things which are not seen.* For the things which are seen are temporary, but the things which are not seen are eternal" (2 Corinthians 4:17-18). The enemy will try to discourage you in many different ways. He will tell you that your prayers have no power and you might as well give up praying altogether. Don't listen to him. Keep looking to God.

The right time to submit to God is now. The right time to resist the enemy is now. The right time to live in the freedom Christ has for you is now. The right time to lay down your life in prayer is now. The right time to "stand fast in the Lord" is always now (Philippians 4:1). That means don't stop praying. Know that your prayers count, even the ones that have not yet been answered.

Jesus told a story about a judge "who did not fear God nor regard man" (Luke 18:2). But there was a widow who kept coming to this judge to get justice regarding her adversary. The judge grew weary of her continually pleading with him and decided to help her. In response to this story Jesus said, "*Shall God not avenge His own elect who cry out day and night to Him, though He bears long with them? I tell you that He will avenge them speedily*" (Luke 18:7-8). Too often people give up praying because the answer has not come. But God says to keep praying and never give up.

Don't start a day, or let a day go by, in which you have not prayed. That being said, refuse to entertain guilt or condemnation when you miss having a prayer time in a day or two. That, too, is a ploy of the enemy. Instead, ask God to help you spend time with Him every day in prayer. Determine to follow God's instruction to "*rejoice always, pray without ceasing, in everything give thanks; for this is the will of God in Christ Jesus for you. Do not quench the Spirit. Do not despise prophecies. Test all things; hold fast what is good. Abstain from every form of evil*" (1 Thessalonians 5:16-22).

The enemy is described as a "roaring lion" prowling around and looking for someone to destroy. We have to be vigilant at all times "lest Satan should take advantage of us; for we are not ignorant of his devices" (2 Corinthians 2:11). If our enemy never takes a day off in pursuing his evil plans, then we must not take a day off in resisting him. So stand your ground. Stay firm in all you know of the Lord and His Word. Decide that you will *not* yield anything to the enemy. "*Watch, stand fast in the faith*, be brave, be strong" (1 Corinthians 16:13).

Draw close to God every day and submit to Him. Be ever ready to listen to Him speak to your heart, ready to obey Him in everything, and responsive to pray how He leads you. That means your heart never becomes hard toward God; it is always tender. And you have decided to follow His orders implicitly, just like a good soldier. When you *resist or stand against the enemy,* the promise of God is that the devil "will *flee*" (James 4:7). It's not that he "maybe possibly might." It's that he absolutely will. He has to.

Resist the Enemy by Refusing to Be Discontent

Supplication means more than just asking for something from God.

Supplication means praying until the burden you have on your heart is released into God's hands.

Only in that transfer of your concerns to God will you experience the kind of peace that takes away all discontentment. Supplication requires praying *through* something. It means to *keep praying* until you see the answer or you receive the peace to stop praying—whichever comes first.

God wants you to be content no matter what condition you are in or what is happening in your life. That doesn't mean you have to *stay* in that condition forever. It means you trust that God is not going to *leave* you in that condition forever. With God things are always changing in your life. *He* is unchanging, but you will *not* be. That's because God wants you always becoming more like Him.

How many people have we seen who have hardened their heart toward God because He did not do what they wanted Him to do? *Apostasy* is departing from God and His Word. It's when people give lip service to God but their hearts are hard toward Him. Jesus said, "These people draw near to Me with their mouth, and honor Me with their lips, *but their heart is far from Me*" (Matthew 15:8). God wants to take us on a journey with Him every day, but too often we want it all given to us without the journey. He has so much He wants to do in our lives, but in order to get to where He wants to take us we must travel with Him step by step in a walk of faith with Him. We want everything now instead of being content with where we are and what we have at the moment, knowing God has more for us than we can even imagine.

God wants you to become more and more dependent on Him so He can take you to places you cannot get to without Him. He wants you to trust that He will provide everything you need for the situation you are in. He wants you to believe as Paul did, "My God shall supply all your need according to His riches in glory by Christ Jesus" (Philippians 4:19).

Paul said, *"I have learned in whatever state I am, to be content"* (Philippians 4:11). And the reason he could say that is explained when he said, *"I can do all things through Christ who strengthens me"* (Philippians 4:13). Paul could be content because he knew that Jesus and the Holy Spirit in him would give him the strength to do whatever he needed to. We need to be certain of that as well. It helps us to resist the enemy no matter what is happening.

Resist the Enemy by Remembering the Truth

One of the best ways to submit to God and resist the enemy is to remember what is true and what is not. It is easier to reject the enemy's lies when you know what God's truth is. The opposite of that is *not* knowing God's truth and believing any lie the enemy tells you. That's why you must know the Word of God well.

Here are a few things to always remember that will help you cling to God and resist the enemy.

Remember this: God loves you more than you know and has a wonderful plan for your life. When you follow Him completely and surrender your life to Him, He enables you to become all He created you to be.

Remember this: The enemy hates you and despises all that God wants to do in your life. He has a plan for your life too, and that is to control you for his purposes and destroy you. He will do all he can to make that happen through his lies and deception.

Remember this: God has given you dominion power on the earth for His purposes.
Remember this: The enemy wants that power for himself for his own purposes.

Remember this: God wants to use you to accomplish His will and glorify Him, while blessing you at the same time.
Remember this: The enemy wants to use your life to glorify himself and destroy you in the process.

Remember this: God has given you a free will, and He waits each day for you to invite Him to work powerfully in your life.
Remember this: The enemy doesn't wait to be invited. He will work in your life unless he is stopped. He wants you to reject God and open up to him instead.

Remember this: It is impossible for God to lie. God only speaks the truth, and He gives us His Word on that.
Remember this: The enemy is the father of all lies. He controls people by enticing them to believe the lies he tells them.

Keep in mind that the enemy is always planning evil. The only thing that restrains him are the prayers of the saints—the prayer warriors. Don't allow this aspect to become vague to you. We can pray anytime, day or night, wherever we are, and that is what we must do on a moment's notice when we are prompted by the Holy Spirit to do so. We cannot ignore those promptings.
Keep in mind that we must have time alone with God in order to communicate our heart to Him and listen to Him communicate

His heart to *us*. Our time alone with God is when we are empowered and filled afresh by the Holy Spirit in us, just as Jesus was. It's when our mind and soul are renewed and strengthened. It's when we receive greater clarity and can receive the guidance, discernment, wisdom, and revelation we need.

Keep in mind that believers everywhere are experiencing the same things that *we* are experiencing. God's Word says of the enemy that we are to "resist him, steadfast in the faith, knowing that the same sufferings are experienced by your brotherhood in the world" (1 Peter 5:9). We are not alone in what we are facing.

Keep in mind that it doesn't matter how strong the enemy is. God is greater. The power of God's Spirit in us is far stronger than that of the enemy.

Keep in mind that *we* are resisting the enemy whenever we pray. When we stand strong by submitting to God, the enemy must flee from us. That is why we must always be ready to do battle with the enemy in prayer. We must remember that we are not going into territory the enemy owns. We are taking back territory the enemy has stolen.

PRAYER FOR THE
PRAYER WARRIOR

LORD, help me to submit myself to You in every possible way. Show me any place in my life where I am not doing that. I don't ever want to seek friendship with the world because I value friendship with You far above all else. Reveal any pride in me so I can repent of it. Cause that recognition to bring the grief and mourning to my soul that it should. I refuse all pride and rebellion in me against You and recognize that they are traits of the enemy. I don't want to ever go against Your will and cooperate with the enemy in any way. I want to resist him in every way possible so that You will not resist me.

Help me to "abhor what is evil" and "cling to what is good" (Romans 12:9). Help me to neither resist You "nor give place to the devil" (Ephesians 4:27). I became Yours the day I received You as Lord over my life, and therefore I cannot be controlled by the enemy in any way.

Help me to resist all lies of the enemy and not allow him to convince me that I am disqualified in any way from being the powerful prayer warrior You have called me to be. I refuse to allow the enemy to talk me into giving up on praying. I will not let him threaten me with my past or make me discontent with where I am now or what I have not yet done. Enable me to resist the enemy in every possible way so he will flee from me. Don't let me be "overcome by evil," but help me to "overcome evil with good" (Romans 12:21). You are the rock on which I stand, and I will not be moved. Thank You, Jesus, that because You laid down Your life for me, I am more than a conqueror through You.

Lord, help me to be the most effective prayer warrior possible. Teach me to understand the authority You have given me in prayer. Enable me to use that authority to break down strongholds the enemy would attempt to establish in my life and in the lives of others whom You put on my heart. I don't want my prayers to be hindered or weakened in any way. Show me what I need to do so that my prayers will have the greatest impact.

In Jesus' name I pray.

You will light my lamp;
the Lord my God will enlighten my darkness.
For by You I can run against a troop,
by my God I can leap over a wall.
As for God, His way is perfect;
the word of the Lord is proven;
He is a shield to all who trust in Him.

PSALM 18:28-30

11

SEE WHAT'S HAPPENING
FROM GOD'S PERSPECTIVE

I had an amazingly dedicated band of intercessors meeting at my house a number of years back. There were six of us, including me, who met faithfully every Tuesday morning. All were strong believers of great faith—solid prayer warriors—who established boundaries in the spirit realm that the enemy could not cross. We not only prayed for ourselves, our families, and people who requested specific prayer, but also situations we knew needed the penetration of God's kingdom and power into them. We had seen such answers to prayer that the only possible explanation for them was that God had done something miraculous. We prayed for three to four hours each time we met. We meant business. That's because we were in the family business—that is, our heavenly Father's family business. We knew we were called. And we were led.

One particular Tuesday morning there were only three of us at prayer. Two members were out of town, and one was very sick with a lung infection and had been admitted to the hospital two days before and was still in intensive care. When I called the hospital to check on Roz that morning just before prayer meeting, she sounded terrible. The congestion in her respiratory system had so invaded her lungs that I didn't even recognize her voice. She could barely talk, and it sounded as though she could barely breathe as well. She said she was getting worse and not better.

I told Suzy and Jan, the other two women at the meeting, what Roz had said. I read from the Word of God, and we had a time of worship the way we always did at the beginning of every prayer meeting. We prayed immediately for Roz and asked God to help us see what was happening from His perspective. Was she on the road to recovery or was she really getting worse? We prayed for a while, yet none of us felt at all released to stop praying for her. I sensed from the Lord that we actually needed to go to the hospital and pray for her there. The other two prayer warriors immediately agreed.

At the hospital, once we were in Roz's room, we sensed right away we were facing an enormous battle in the spirit realm. We immediately began to worship God and thank Jesus that He is our healer. We prayed for healing, but we all had a vision that this was more than just an illness. It may have started out as an illness or imbalance in her body, but the enemy had taken it to a new level. I am not saying she wasn't sick, but that the enemy was not only keeping her from getting better, she was getting worse. I am also not saying we should blame everything on the enemy, but we should always ask God to show us what is happening from His perspective so we know how to pray. We prayed that no weapon of the enemy formed against Roz would prosper in any way. (There is that great Scripture again—Isaiah 54:17.)

When we first began praying for Roz, she was very weak, her breathing was labored, and she could hardly talk above a whisper. But the more we continued to pray, the more she showed signs of renewed strength right before our eyes. While we were praying, I felt strongly led to remove the numerous bouquets of flowers from her room and put them in the hall outside her door. We continued praying for about twenty minutes, even though nurses came into her room to check on her. They seemed totally fine with what we were doing. By the end of our prayer time she showed remarkable improvement. Her strength had revived, she was breathing normally, and her countenance had visibly changed. She became more animated and talked freely and clearly. She vigorously described how much better she felt. She said, "This is a miracle." And we all agreed. By the time we left, she seemed totally well. The entire room felt different. We thought she may have to stay awhile in the hospital to make certain she was recovered and out of danger, but to our surprise she was released to go home the next morning.

Just a few days afterward I received a letter in the mail addressed to me, Suzy, and Jan. And this is one of the reasons I have related this story. I have kept this letter in my prayer book all these years— that's the book where I write all prayer requests that I pray about, as well as answers to prayer. Just the other day, as I was writing this chapter you are reading, I remembered the letter and went looking for it. I knew I would never have thrown it away, yet I hadn't seen it in years and wasn't sure it was still there. But then I found it in one of the side pockets of that old leather prayer book.

I wish you could see it because it is an official-looking typed letter that appears as if it could have come from some branch of the military. But it didn't. At least not in *this* world.

This is what she wrote:

September 11, 1996
Stormie Omartian, General
The God Squad
Nashville, Tennessee

Dear General Omartian,

When you, Admiral Martinez, and Colonel Williamson entered the Critical Care Unit, I was being held prisoner and "All Hell Broke Loose" of me when you prayed. Praise God! Your weapons of touch, prayer, and the spoken Word were impossible to defeat.

Thank you for your obedience to our Commander-in-Chief to launch such a powerfully, strategic and tactical maneuver on my behalf. I will forever be grateful for the rescue. Thank you.

In His service, with love,
Roz Thompson, Soldier in the Army of the Lord

The cleverness of the letter made us all laugh. But here we are, all friends and fellow prayer warriors years later. Only now we see the battle far more clearly than we did back then. We have greater knowledge about what the Word says about the opposition we are facing. And we know we will never back down.

God wants us to see things from His perspective. I'm sure He doesn't want us to see everything He sees, but certainly He wants us to see more than we do. So we must ask Him to reveal everything we need to understand in order to pray powerfully. When He does show us something we have not seen before, it can be life-changing.

Seeing things from God's perspective helps us to pray God's will and to better understand God's timing of events. And when our prayers aren't answered the way we expect they would, it helps us to trust without hesitation that God knows what He is doing far better than *we* know how we think things should be done.

God is referred to as the One "who gives life to the dead and *calls those things which do not exist as though they did*" (Romans 4:17). Isn't that the best? God can call into existence something that is not existing at the time. For example, He can bring a solution to an impossible situation that we could not even imagine. He can bring life into something that has died. He can make love that has died between two people come alive again. He can take the broken parts of our life and make them whole. He can bring good out of a bad situation when it doesn't seem possible. We may not be able to even imagine how He will do it, but we don't have to. We just have to believe He *can*.

Thank God that He is not limited by what we think or imagine.

When we are attacked by the enemy and we see nothing but disaster in the situation, we have to remember that the solution may be far beyond what we can envision. He has done exactly that for me countless times. When we ask Him to, He can reveal things to us through His Spirit, and the Spirit knows everything (1 Corinthians 2:9-10). When we ask the Holy Spirit to reveal what God wants to do in a situation, He will.

God wants us to always keep eternity in mind. That is *His* perspective after all, and He wants *us* to see it. When we do, it helps us to understand that "the sufferings of this present time are not worthy to be compared with the glory which shall be revealed in us" (Romans 8:18). Our suffering here pales in comparison to the great things He has waiting for us. Understanding that changes our perspective on everything.

That's why when our prayers are not answered the way we hoped they would be, we cannot question it. We must always keep in mind that He is God and we are not. That is definitely *His* perspective and it must be ours as well. God is not a genie we can command. Not even close.

So even if we pray for a sick believer, for example, and that person not only does not recover, but dies, we must ask God to help us see the situation from His perspective. There is great comfort in knowing what He sees with regard to our eternal future. Ask Him to give you a glimpse of your eternal future. He will give you a vision, no matter how brief, and your life will never be the same.

It is written of God's people who were rebellious to His ways that "God has given them a spirit of stupor, eyes that they should not see and ears that they should not hear, to this very day" (Romans 11:8). Surely the One who gave them a spirit of stupor and blind eyes to the truth and ears deaf to His voice, can give *us*—whose hearts are soft toward Him and open to His voice—the ability to see and understand what He wants to reveal to us.

Jesus illustrated that a godly leader is one who helps and serves others. The real qualification for service to God is an attitude of the heart that is seen in action. The last thing you would expect of Jesus is that He needed to wash His disciples' feet, but that is what He did in order to show them how to serve God by serving others. Every time you pray as a prayer warrior, it is as if you are washing the feet of Jesus. You are submitting to Him as His servant and doing what most pleases Him—serving others.

From God's Perspective, We Can See a Second Chance for Greatness

God is the God of second chances. We would all be dead if that weren't true. If you've made big mistakes or bad decisions and feel you may have lost your chance to do something great for God, know that this is not true. If you've been far away from the right path for too long and don't think you can ever really get back on it again, that is also not true. The truth is that the moment you reconnect your life to the Lord and *rededicate* your life to His service, He will revive you again. You can come back from trouble.

King David, who got off the path God had for him and into as much sin and trouble as anyone could—with adultery, deception, and murder on his record—said, "You who have done great things; O God, who is like You? You, who have shown me great and severe troubles, *shall revive me again*, and bring me up again from the depths of the earth. *You shall increase my greatness*, and *comfort me on every side*" (Psalm 71:19-21).

If God can do that for His chosen king, a man after His own heart who sinned terribly, He can do that for you. We too often see ourselves from our past. God sees us from our future. We see ourselves from our failure. God sees us from our purpose.

Isn't it encouraging to know that no matter how far we have sunk down under the weight of our circumstances, we can rise again? We can come back from trouble. We can do whatever God has called us to do. We can have a second chance at greatness.

We must ask God to show us our future from *His* perspective and not try to control it from our own.

One of the greatest stories in the Bible is how Abraham traveled with his large family and all his cattle and servants to where God was leading him. When Abraham's family and his nephew, Lot's, family had grown far too numerous to stay together in the same place, they decided to divide up and go separate ways in order for the land to sustain them. Abraham gave Lot the opportunity to choose his land first. The problem was that Lot didn't pray and ask God where *He* wanted him to go. He chose *what appeared to be* the best land for himself and his family.

The land Lot chose turned out to be Sodom, a city God eventually destroyed. When that happened, Lot and his wife and daughters were forced to flee, and they lost everything they had in the process. On the way Lot's wife disobeyed the instruction God gave to them to not look back, and that step of disobedience destroyed her.

Talk about taking matters into their own hands—a family trait, obviously—Lot's daughters decided to do just that. In order to save themselves and their family line from extinction, one night when their father was passed out from too much wine, they took advantage of him. You can see why the father wanted to drink himself into a stupor. He had lost everything, including his wife, and he was in a foreign land and afraid for his life. He had chosen what he thought the best land, and it turned out to be a curse that brought nothing but disaster.

To make a not very long story even mercifully shorter, the two girls ended up getting pregnant by their inebriated father. Isn't it amazing what people will do when they are desperate and don't turn to God for guidance? As a result, the oldest daughter bore a son named Moab— who became father of the Moabites. The young-est daughter bore a son name Ben-Ammi—who became the father of the Ammonites. The origin of the Moabites and Ammonites—enemies of God's people—began with Lot's daughters committing incest with their father in order to have children. There is no limit to how low people can get who do not seek God. (See the story of Lot in the book of Genesis, chapters 13–19.)

Abraham, on the other hand, went where God told him to go and God blessed him wherever he went.

In my own life, I experienced something similar when my husband wanted to move from California to Tennessee. I didn't want to go because I couldn't imagine leaving my family, friends, church, and a lifestyle that at least I understood. I was against it until I fasted and prayed and asked God to show me this decision from *His* perspective. He clearly revealed it one day on a trip to Tennessee. I saw from God's perspective that we were supposed to move. So we went home, put our house up for sale, went back to Tennessee, and bought a house before ours had even sold—which is considered an unwise thing to do by any business advisor. But we knew we had to move as soon as possible. And the reason, I feel God showed me, is that there would be an earthquake and our house would not be safe in it.

So we moved to Tennessee without selling the California house—a very scary thing to do—and just a few months afterward our house was destroyed in the Northridge earthquake of 1994. My family and I were stunned with what would probably have happened to us had we stayed in California. We have never forgotten how we listened to God and were blessed for it. Because the house had not sold, we lost a lot of money on it, in spite of having earthquake insurance, which we found out only pays for what the house is worth at the time of the earthquake. (My advice is to buy a strong magnifying glass in order to read fine print before you sign any contract.) Nevertheless, we were grateful to be alive and thankful we had taken out all of our furniture and possessions before it was destroyed.

When my children and I went back to Los Angeles to look at the damage, we cried thinking what it would have been like to be there at the time of the earthquake. We were grateful for what God had done. All of our friends and neighbors agreed it was by far the worst quake they had ever been in, and I could tell from their faces and the way they talked about it that this was true. Had we not asked God to give us His perspective on the situation, we could have lost more than possessions. We could have lost our lives. I am not saying that those who were in the earthquake did not hear from God. That is not true at all. They were protected in the earthquake and their houses were not destroyed as ours was.

It is always better to have what God wants you to have than to strive for something else, because what God gives you brings no curse with it. We have been greatly blessed living in Tennessee in ways we never dreamed possible. It was the best decision for all of us because it was God's will and we listened.

I know a man who had been out of work for a while and prayed for a job. When a good job opened up for him, he took it and committed to that company to do the work. However, soon afterward he was offered what he thought was a *better* job at another company. So he reneged on the first job commitment and took the second job instead. A few months later the second job offer he accepted was canceled completely and the first job he had deserted was already filled by someone else. He ended up losing both jobs because he didn't seek the leading of the Holy Spirit and do the right thing. He didn't keep his commitment to his first job offer, which was an answer to his prayers. And he didn't pray about the second job offer. He just took it without question. The first job he deserted turned out to be with a company that became very successful. The man who took his place at that job had enormous success.

When we follow the leading of the Holy Spirit, we end up in a place of safety and blessing. When we insist on our own way—an opportunistic way of life causing us to grab what appears to be the greatest perceived opportunity for ourselves instead of what God is leading us to do—we don't get to experience God's best. We must be able to see things from God's perspective. And that takes asking God to show us the truth of a situation from His standpoint.

From God's Perspective, We See the Importance of Our Prayers

Jesus said, "Unless one is born again, he cannot see the kingdom of God" (John 3:3). That is the beginning of seeing things from God's perspective. Unless we are born again, and anchored in His Word, and following the leading of His Holy Spirit in us, we can't understand how to advance the kingdom of God on earth in prayer.

One of the things we see from God's Word is that we reap what we sow. This is a hard-and-fast law of the universe. The only way this is not true is when we confess and repent of the bad things we have sown. Even then, sometimes we have to reap the bad crop before we can reap the new crop planted with good seeds. We can appeal to God's grace so that we won't receive what we deserve, but that cannot be manipulated. God decides.

The Bible says, "Do not be deceived, *God is not mocked; for whatever a man sows, that he will also reap. For he who sows to his flesh will of the flesh reap corruption, but he who sows to the Spirit will of the Spirit reap everlasting life*" (Galatians 6:7-8). When we are praying for people or situations, we have to keep in mind that the trouble going on in their lives could be because of what they have sown in the flesh. If they are bearing the consequences for that, you must pray that their eyes be opened to see from God's perspective. You can't just pray that God will fix something that can't be fixed without their eyes being opened to the truth. They must see their need for repentance so they can receive forgiveness from the Lord. We are not allowed to ignore that fact.

The truth is, we reap what we sow in prayer, just as in everything else we do in life. When we are planting seeds of prayer, we can't put God on our timetable for reaping. We must simply depend on God's promise that we *will* reap what we sow.

Refuse to be discouraged when you don't see the results you want right away. You are on *God's* timetable; He is not on yours. He guarantees that you will reap a harvest. He didn't say exactly how long it would take. If we keep on with great faith, spending our life sowing seeds in prayer, we are sure to reap the harvest according to what we have sown.

In certain cases we may not see the harvest from the seeds of prayer we have planted in our lifetime, but because our prayers don't die, their effect will continue on after we have gone to be with the Lord. Remember that bowl in heaven I mentioned that contains the prayers of the saints? That means our prayers don't just barely make it to the ceiling before they evaporate. God not only hears those prayers, but He keeps them so they will continue to have an effect. There is not a timer on our prayers that causes them to be ineffective after a certain amount of time has passed. Can you imagine hearing a voice from heaven saying, "Beep! Your prayers for your relationships at work have expired."

Every time you pray, a seed is planted. The Bible says in response to sowing and reaping, "*Let us not grow weary while doing good*, for in due season we shall reap if we do not lose heart. Therefore, as we have opportunity, let us do good to all, especially to those who are of the household of faith" (Galatians 6:9-10). One of the good things we can do is to pray.

When you see things from God's perspective, your life as a prayer warrior will never be drudgery. You will see that you are called and enabled by the Holy Spirit. As you invite the Holy Spirit to lead you, your prayers will always be alive. Your prayer life will continue to be exciting as you feel His presence leading you. And you will be amazed how often God will put the same thing on the hearts of different people and you will be a team that He has assembled.

However, that being said, if there are times when you feel you may be the one person praying for a particular urgent situation—because you are concerned that you may be the only one listening for His voice about a certain thing—ask God to awaken other prayer warriors to join you. I know He does that. I have heard their testimonies to that affect. I, too, have been awakened with a burden God has put on my heart, only to find out later that others had the same experience.

Remember the football analogy in chapter 4? That is a way to see things from God's perspective when you are praying. You leap into a situation in prayer and God shows you how to take it in the opposite direction from the way it is headed. We can do that for other people. We can do it for one another. We can do it for ourselves. When a situation or person is going in the wrong direction—that is, against the will of God—He will show you how to pray and take it in the direction of victory for the glory of God.

It's teamwork. You may be alone in a room when you are praying, but countless other members are on the prayer warrior team who are working together to keep the enemy from achieving his goal.

We must pray that we can understand God's purpose for us in everything we do—including pray. Pray that God will give you insight into His Word every time you read it. Pray that the Holy Spirit will continually enlighten your understanding. Ask God to help you understand His calling on your life and to give you a vision of what He wants to do. You need that. If you don't ask God to help you see things from *His* perspective, there will be times when you may not understand how to pray at all.

From God's Perspective, We Understand the Last Days

What will it be like in the end-time? See if Paul's letter to Timothy describes anything that sounds at all familiar to you. He said, "In the last days perilous times will come: For men will be lovers of themselves, lovers of money, boasters, proud, blasphemers, disobedient to parents, unthankful, unholy, unloving, unforgiving, slanderers, without self-control, brutal, despisers of good, traitors, headstrong, haughty, lovers of pleasure rather than lovers of God, having a form of godliness but denying its power. And from such people turn away!" (2 Timothy 3:1-5). Can we doubt from this perspective that we are in the last days?

It goes on to say that some people will be "always learning and never able to come to the knowledge of the truth" (2 Timothy 3:7). These people will pretend to be Christians but deny the Holy Spirit—the power of God—who *dwells* in us, *transforms* us and *works* through us. They will deny that Jesus rose from the dead. They will deny the Bible as the inspired Word of God. I heard all of this on a news program last week.

Paul said that in the end-time people will turn away from the truth. "They will not endure sound doctrine, but according to their own desires, because they have itching ears, they will heap up for themselves teachers" (2 Timothy 4:3). When you see this kind of unrighteousness flourishing around you, you have to know that this was predicted.

But just because it has been foretold in the Bible that the days will be evil and people will do terrible things doesn't mean we don't pray about it. We must continue to pray for our children, our family members, and the people God puts on our heart. We must pray more than ever that believers will be protected and not swept up in such evil things.

You must keep praying always as God leads you so that you can say as Paul said to Timothy, "*I have fought the good fight, I have finished the race, I have kept the faith.* Finally, there is laid up for me the crown of righteousness, which the Lord, the righteous Judge, will give to me on that Day, and not to me only but also to all who have loved His appearing" (2 Timothy 4:7-8). A prayer warrior always fights the good fight in prayer.

Even when times get ugly or hard, remember that you have a

"crown of righteousness" laid up for you in heaven. Because of Jesus, you are acquitted totally and the righteousness of Jesus is imparted to you. The enemy was defeated the moment Jesus was resurrected from the dead because death and hell could not hold Him.

Ask God to show you the truth about what is going on in the world. Don't just read newspapers or nightly news programs on TV that tell you only what *they* want you to know. You are not getting the full picture from *any* of them. Only God can show you the whole picture because it can only be accurately seen from *His* perspective. He knows the beginning and the end and everything in between.

The greatest story in the Bible about seeing things from God's perspective is the one about Elisha, the prophet, and his servant during the war between Israel and Syria. Elisha had been prophetically advising the king of Israel how to avoid the traps the Syrians had set for them. When the Syrian army found out it was Elisha telling Israel's king of their secret plans—because God had revealed them to him—the Syrian army surrounded the city where Elisha was so they could capture him.

When the servant got up one morning and saw the Syrian army surrounding the city, he desperately asked Elisha what they should do. Elisha was calm in the midst of the siege because he could see what was happening from God's perspective. The servant was frightened because he could not.

Elisha responded to his servant with his now famous words, "*Do not fear, for those who are with us are more than those who are with them*" (2 Kings 6:16). Elisha prayed, and said, "'LORD, I pray, open his eyes that he may see.' Then the LORD opened the eyes of the young man, and he saw. And behold, *the mountain was full of horses and chariots of fire all around Elisha*" (2 Kings 6:16-17). When the eyes of the servant were opened and he saw what was happening in the spirit realm, it changed everything for him.

We all need that vision from the Lord. We need to see it in His

Word, for that fortifies and emboldens us, but there are also specific times when we need special revelation from God. That can make all the difference. When you are in an intense struggle in prayer, ask God to show you what is happening from His perspective. Having clear perspective from the Lord allows you to see what you are dealing with and how God wants you to pray.

Pray for your eyes to be open to the truth in *every* situation and reveal the strategies of the enemy. Pray to be able to see into the invisible spiritual realm. We want our spiritual eyes to be opened when we are praying for people or situations. We need to know when something bad happens if it is an attack of the enemy or the result of corrupt seeds sown in the flesh.

When Elisha's servant saw that the hills all around were crowded with horses and chariots of fire, he understood that they were not alone, for the angels in God's spiritual army were there to protect them.

God's army of angels protects us too.

An angel delivered Peter out of prison (Acts 12). An angel told Paul his prayers had been answered for the safety of his crew in the storm while aboard a ship (Acts 27:21-26). Angels offer up the prayers of believers like you and me. "Then another angel, having a golden censer, came and stood at the altar. He was given much incense, that he should offer it *with the prayers of all the saints* upon the golden altar which was before the throne. And the smoke of the incense, with *the prayers of the saints*, ascended before God from the angel's hand" (Revelation 8:3-4).

Don't you love that?

Jesus commands both the army of angels in heaven and the army of believers on earth and coordinates them so that the heavenly army helps the earthly army. "To which of the angels has He ever said: 'Sit at My right hand, till I make Your enemies Your footstool'? Are they not all *ministering spirits sent forth to minister for those who will inherit salvation*?" (Hebrews 1:13-14).

When prayer warriors pray, angels help us in our battle against the enemy. Jesus said, "Do you think that I cannot now pray to My Father, and He will provide Me with more than *twelve legions of angels*?" (Matthew 26:53).

We don't have to be afraid that God has left us here to fight alone. Nothing could be further from the truth.

From God's Perspective, We See the Right Thing to Do

Noah heard from God and was led to do something that made no sense from an earthly perspective. "Noah, *being divinely warned of things not yet seen*, moved with godly fear, prepared an ark for the saving of his household, by which he condemned the world and became heir of the righteousness which is according to faith" (Hebrews 11:7). The pure evidence of Noah's faith and godly perspective was that where he built the ark (a giant boat) was nowhere near any body of water. Seeing from God's perspective helped him do what he needed to do. And as a result, it saved his life along with the lives of his family members and many animals.

When Jesus talked to His disciples about what was to come, He said, "They will deliver you up to tribulation and kill you, and you will be hated by all nations for My name's sake" (Matthew 24:9). That must have been frightening to hear, but it also must have helped them endure when they saw it all come to pass. It encouraged them to do what they needed to do.

This is where the world is headed now. Christians have been persecuted in the past since Jesus was crucified, and now it will continue to get worse. In every arena you look, Jesus is being crowded out and His people are being mocked and persecuted.

Recognize the times we are in. See what is happening in your nation. Listen to *the watchmen on your walls*—godly men and women who see what is happening in our nation and in other nations and who pray accordingly. The enemy is winning many battles each day and night, and we cannot sit by and let it happen.

Only God knows when Jesus will return for His people. And He has told us to stand strong to the end. You never know the extent of what God will do in response to your prayers. Lives can be saved everywhere, in every way possible.

Ask God for His perspective when you are praying for others. How does He want you to pray? How is the Holy Spirit leading you?

Jeremiah had prayed to God for understanding about a situation. The territory Israel was about to possess was still in enemy hands. Jeremiah praised God and said, "Ah, Lord GOD! Behold, You have made the heavens and the earth by Your great power and out-stretched arm. *There is nothing too hard for You*" (Jeremiah 32:17).

God told Jeremiah that if he called on Him, He would show him things he couldn't possible know otherwise (Jeremiah 33:3). God is saying the same thing to us today. We can call on Him and ask Him to show us things from His perspective, and He will show us things that we could not possibly know without Him revealing it to us. We absolutely must have this kind of insight in order to be victorious in our spiritual warfare and in our life. We cannot pray as powerfully and effectively as we need to pray without having revelation from the Lord.

Your prayers can open doors for someone's salvation into God's kingdom for eternity. Your prayers can save countless people from suffering and disaster, including yourself and your loved ones. Your prayers may save lives that would otherwise be destroyed, or prevent terrible things from happening that the enemy has planned. If you could prevent good people from certain horrific death, wouldn't you pray if you knew it would save them? Of course you would. You would not have read this far if you didn't believe that prayer can make a difference—and specifically *your* prayers can make a difference—in this world.

Your prayers are vital. Every prayer can save a life, change a life, spare a life, or redeem a life.

We must have the perspective that our walk with God on earth is

like a race, and we are to "lay aside every weight, and the sin which
so easily ensnares us, and let us run with endurance the race that is
set before us, *looking unto Jesus, the author and finisher of our faith*,
who for the joy that was set before Him endured the cross, despis-
ing the shame, and has sat down at the right hand of the throne of
God" (Hebrews 12:1-2). We must think of what Jesus endured for us
so that we don't become weary and discouraged in our souls because
of our struggles here on earth that we endure for Him.

    When God took the apostle John up to heaven to see things from
His perspective, John described it saying, "I heard a loud voice saying in heaven, 'Now salvation, and strength, and the kingdom of
our God, and the power of His Christ have come, for *the accuser
of our brethren, who accused them before our God day and night, has
been cast down. And *they overcame him by the blood of the Lamb and
by the word of their testimony*, and they did not love their lives to the
death'" (Revelation 12:10-11). That perspective changed everything
for John, and it should for us as well.

    Jesus has *called us* "out of darkness into His marvelous light"
(1 Peter 2:9). We are to *walk worthy of our calling* (Ephesians 4:1).
We are set aside for special service to the Lord and will receive God's
special blessings and favor. We are to *grow in purity* (Ephesians 4:17-
31) and *forgiveness* (Ephesians 4:32). We are to *walk in the fullness
of the Holy Spirit* (Ephesians 5:1-21). We are *equipped* because He
equips us (Ephesians 4:11-16).

    God has called us out of darkness into His perfect light because
we are His *special people created for the purpose of proclaiming His
praise*. We believers are considered holy. This means our authority
as a believer corresponds to our walk in purity as His special people
who proclaim His praises and worship Him. Worship is absolutely
necessary in order to see advancement of God's kingdom on earth.

    Israel was only able to do battle through purifying themselves
and doing battle in worship first. It is the same for us today. We will

only do great things for God and take territory for His kingdom as we grow in humble and heartfelt worship of Him and live His way. And that is the only way we can see things from God's perspective.

God wants us to walk closely with Him in prayer. He wants us to worship Him and praise His name. We are a royal priesthood, which means we are kings and priests (Revelation 1:5-6). And we not only walk with Him in His "marvelous light," but we go to war with Him and for Him against the forces of darkness. We believers are a holy nation formed from every nation and race of all who believe in Jesus. We are "His own special people" who are "the called" who are to proclaim praise to Him wherever we are and wherever we go. It is an honor and a privilege.

God sees all that you do. He sees how you pray. He sees your heart for Him and others. "*God is not unjust to forget your work and labor of love* which you have shown toward His name, in that you have ministered to the saints, and do minister" (Hebrews 6:10). We cannot lose heart because we see horrible things that will happen in the end-time. We must keep praying as faithful prayer warriors in God's army. "*We desire that each one of you show the same diligence to the full assurance of hope until the end,* that you do not become sluggish, but imitate those who through faith and patience inherit the promises" (Hebrews 6:11-12). "Thanks be to God, who gives us the victory through our Lord Jesus Christ" (1 Corinthians 15:57).

Jesus knows the enemy. He understands the battle. Because He has overcome, so will we.

PRAYER FOR THE
PRAYER WARRIOR

LORD, help me lay aside every concern and burden in my heart and reject all temptation to be sidetracked from what You have called me to do, so that I can run the race You have set before me. Keep my eyes focused on You at all times. Thank You that You have saved me and are perfecting me by the power of Your Spirit. I invite You to lead me every day so that I will stay on the path You have for me. Help me to be counted a good and faithful soldier in Your army of saints who battle in prayer every day, and who wield the sword of the Spirit—Your Word—as a weapon against all the plans of the enemy.

Just as You endured the cross and the suffering that went with it because You saw the glory and joy set before You at the right hand of Your Father God, help me to endure what I must for the joy set before me of knowing You have defeated the enemy and I will spend eternity with You. Thank You for the joy of knowing we win because You have conquered death and defeated hell.

Lord, I thank You that You are the God of second chances, and You have given me a second chance to do something great for You. No matter what I have done or what has happened in my past, You will still use me for Your purposes because I have committed my life to You in every way. Thank You that You provide a way back from trouble. I submit my life to You again. Help me to never take things into my own hands but to look to You for direction.

Enable me to see things from Your perspective so I always

know how to pray and what the right thing is to do. Help me also to see this time in the world—that in light of Your Word seems to be closing in on the last days—so that I will know how to pray. I don't ever want to be a person who is "always learning and never able to come to the knowledge of the truth" (2 Timothy 3:7). I don't ever want to deny the power of Your Holy Spirit in me as Your Word says many will do in the last days. Keep me from ever turning away from the truth (2 Timothy 4:3). I want to be able to say that "I have fought the good fight, I have finished the race, I have kept the faith" and now there is "laid up for me a crown of righteousness" that You will give to me and all who love You on that final day when we go to be with You (2 Timothy 4:7-8).

Because of You, Lord, I can "glory in tribulations, knowing that tribulation produces perseverance; and perseverance, character; and character, hope" (Romans 5:3-4). And I know I will never be disappointed by putting my hope in You because Your love has been poured out in my heart by the Holy Spirit in me, who is the guarantee of my great future with You (Romans 5:3-5).

In Jesus' name I pray.

Call to Me, and I will answer you,
and show you great and mighty things,
which you do not know.

JEREMIAH 33:3

Powerful Prayers for Spiritual Warfare

1. Prayer for a Covering of Protection
2. Prayer for Deliverance from Evil
3. Prayer for Healing
4. Prayer for Personal Guidance and Discernment
5. Prayer for Provision
6. Prayer for Victory over Enemy Attack
7. Prayer for the Hearts of Children
8. Prayer for a Safe Place and an End to Violence
9. Prayer for an End to Confusion
10. Prayer for Freedom from Enemy Harassment
11. Prayer for Your Leaders
12. Prayer for Others to Be Saved
13. Prayer for Racial Unity
14. Prayer for Exaltation of God
15. Prayer for Those Who Suffer Persecution
16. Prayer for a Clean Heart and Humble Spirit
17. Prayer for Strength in the Battle
18. Prayer for Peace in Relationships
19. Prayer for Deliverance and Freedom
20. Prayer for Serious Situations in the World

12

Pray the Prayers Every
Prayer Warrior Must Know

Reading about prayer is good. Talking about prayer is great. But neither accomplishes anything if we are not actually praying. We have to pray every day about whatever must be covered. And because the source of all our power in prayer is the Lord, if we are not spending time with Him in prayer then we are losing power. We can't afford to lose power with so formidable an enemy opposing all that God wants to do *in* us, *through* us, and *around* us.

The previous 11 chapters were about how to *become* a strong prayer warrior. In this last chapter, I have provided important prayers every prayer warrior must know. These areas of prayer focus are important to your life, the lives of those for whom you pray, and for advancing the kingdom of God on earth. But that doesn't mean you have to pray all of them every day. Not at all. You could choose one a day or one a week. Pray these prayers as you feel led by the Holy Spirit. He will show you what to pray about when you ask Him.

Every prayer is worded so you can pray it for yourself, another person, or a number of people. Just insert the appropriate name in the space provided and select the pronouns accordingly. In every prayer, the sword of the Spirit is prominent to bring maximum protection and power. This helps you resist the encroachment of the enemy in *your* life and the lives of *others*. Each prayer will affect the people and situations around you for the greatest good, stop the plans of the enemy from succeeding, help you and others to stand strong in the battle when things shake around you, and accomplish the will of God. That is not a bad return for so little investment of time.

The twenty important areas of prayer focus included here are where the enemy will most likely attack us and others. You will undoubtedly think of more, so as you pray, have a pad of paper and a pen beside you in order to write down what God speaks to your heart. It doesn't have to be elaborate. Just a simple reminder of how the Holy Spirit is impressing you to pray. You don't have to pray about everything every day. That would be too much, and that is not a burden God has given you. You are simply to pray for yourself, your family, and the people and situations God puts on your heart.

Let your prayers be initiated by your love for God and your willingness to serve Him. Answer the call to be His prayer warrior in order to see His will done on earth. The Holy Spirit will lead you, so stay in close contact with Him. Invite Him to prompt your heart, mind, and spirit *when* to pray, *how* to pray, and *what* to pray. And when He brings a person, people, or a set of circumstances to mind, check these prayers to see if one of them might be a good starting point.

There is tremendous power in the prayers of a prayer warrior, so "do not grow weary in doing good" (2 Thessalonians 3:13). Often the greatest good you can do is to pray and *keep on* praying whether you see the answers right away or not. Praying as God's prayer warrior is an excellent way to get to the end of your life knowing you have fought the good fight and fulfilled your calling. You don't have to know how every prayer is answered; you just have to believe that God has heard them all and will answer in His way and time.

You just pray. And trust Him to do the rest.

That's what prayer warriors do.

1. Prayer for a Covering of Protection

LORD, I ask You to cover me and my family with Your protection. Surround us with Your angels to keep us from danger, accidents, disease, or any plans of the enemy to harm us. You are my strength and my shield and I trust in You (Psalm 28:7). Thank You that You keep me from harm and will watch over my coming and going both now and in eternity (Psalm 121:8). "You are my hiding place and my shield; I hope in Your word" (Psalm 119:114). Thank You, Lord, that You "will bless the righteous; with favor You will surround him as with a shield" (Psalm 5:12). Thank You that in the time of trouble You will hide me from the enemy in a secret place. You "shall set me high upon a rock" (Psalm 27:5).

Lord, Your Word says that "He who dwells in the secret place of the Most High shall abide under the shadow of the Almighty" (Psalm 91:1). I say that You are my "refuge and my fortress;" You are my God and I will trust in You (Psalm 91:2).

I pray You would also protect (name of person(s) on your heart who needs God's protection). Keep her (him, them) from the hands of the evil one (2 Thessalonians 3:3). Protect her (him, them) from violent men. Wherever the enemy has set a trap, I pray You would rescue her (him, them) out of the snare (Psalm 140:4-6). Thank You that You will deliver her (him, them) "from the snare of the fowler and from the perilous pestilence" (Psalm 91:3). Thank You that You will be a covering so that she (he, they) can take refuge in You, and You will be an impenetrable shield from the enemy (Psalm 91:4).

Thank You that You are our refuge in times of trouble (Nahum 1:7). You are a shield for all who take refuge in You. Help us to remember that You, Lord, are "our refuge and strength, a very present help in trouble" (Psalm 46:1).

In Jesus' name I pray.

You shall not be afraid of the terror by night,
nor of the arrow that flies by day,
nor of the pestilence that walks in darkness,
nor of the destruction that lays waste at noonday.
A thousand may fall at your side,
and ten thousand at your right hand;
but it shall not come near you.
Only with your eyes shall you look, and
see the reward of the wicked.

PSALM 91:5-8

2. Prayer for Deliverance from Evil

LORD, I know evil is all around us, but You have said that those who hide themselves in You will be delivered from the enemy. Help me to hide myself in You. I also pray the same for (name of person or people on your heart who need to be protected or delivered from evil). Thank You that You send angels to guard us and keep us from the plans of the evil one. Lord Jesus, You have said that "everyone practicing evil hates the light and does not come to the light, lest his deeds should be exposed. But he who does the truth comes to the light, that his deeds may be clearly seen, that they have been done in God" (John 3:20-21). Help him (her, us) to always turn away from evil and do all he (she, we) does in the light of Your presence (1 Peter 3:11). Where evil has pursued us, I pray You would break all attempts of the enemy to erect any kind of stronghold or snare. Help us to "abhor what is evil" and "cling to what is good" (Romans 12:9).

Help him (her, us) to "be wise in what is good, and simple concerning evil" (Romans 16:19). Help him (her, us) to "abstain from every form of evil" (1 Thessalonians 5:22). Your Word says, "Blessed is the man who endures temptation; for when he has been approved, he will receive the crown of life which the Lord has promised to those who love Him" (James 1:12). Enable him (her, us) to resist all temptation by the enemy to disobey You and do what should not be done. Help him (her, us) not to be enticed by the enemy in any way.

Thank You, Lord, that You are faithful to establish us on solid ground and guard us from the evil one (2 Thessalonians 3:3). Show us any way in which we have invited the enemy in by not living according to Your will. Thank You, Jesus, that You are the Deliverer who came to set us free from death and hell. Dear Lord, deliver us from evil this day.

In Jesus' name I pray.

> *Because you have made the LORD,*
> *who is my refuge, even the Most High,*
> *your dwelling place, no evil shall befall you,*
> *nor shall any plague come near your dwelling;*
> *for He shall give His angels charge over you,*
> *to keep you in all your ways.*
> *In their hands they shall bear you up,*
> *lest you dash your foot against a stone.*
>
> PSALM 91:9-12

3. Prayer for Healing

LORD, I thank You that You are the God who heals. Thank You, Jesus, that You have "borne our griefs and carried our sorrows" and You were "wounded for our transgressions" and "bruised for our iniquities" and by Your "stripes we are healed" (Isaiah 53:4-5). Thank You that You "took our infirmities and bore our sicknesses" (Matthew 8:17). By the authority given me in the name of Jesus, I pray for healing for (name of person who needs healing). I pray that no plans of the enemy for this person's destruction will succeed. Bring healing to every part of her (his, my) body.

Specifically, I pray for (name specific area of healing that is needed). Cause her (his, my) body to function in the way You created it to so that every part of the body is cleansed of all that should not be there. Give her (him, me) wisdom as to what food to eat, what medicine to take or not take, what health practitioner to see, and what to do to bring and sustain good health. In the name of Jesus I resist all plans of the enemy to inflict infirmity or disease of any kind upon her (him, me).

Lord, You have said in Your Word to "confess your trespasses to one another, and pray for one another, that you may be healed. The effective, fervent prayer of a righteous man avails much" (James 5:16). Where confession of sin is needed, make that apparent so there can be repentance. I know that "a merry heart does good, like medicine, but a broken spirit dries the bones" (Proverbs 17:22). Show me where brokenness and a lack of joy have kept healing away. Whether this infirmity is healed instantly or requires a convalescent period, I give You the glory as our Creator and Healer.

"O LORD my God, I cried out to You, and You healed me" (Psalm 30:2). Thank You that You save those who cry out to You in their trouble and distress, and that You heal them and deliver them from destruction (Psalm 107:19-20). On behalf of (<u>name of person for whom you are praying</u>), I say, "Heal me, O LORD, and I shall be healed; save me, and I shall be saved" (Jeremiah 17:14).

Lord, Your Word says, "Is anyone among you suffering? Let him pray. Is anyone cheerful? Let him sing psalms. Is anyone among you sick? Let him call for the elders of the church, and let them pray over him, anointing him with oil in the name of the Lord. *And the prayer of faith will save the sick, and the Lord will raise him up*" (James 5:13-15). Help us to pray the prayer of faith. Help us to confess our sins and pray for one another so we can be healed (James 5:16).

In Jesus' name I pray.

Bless the LORD, O my soul,
and forget not all His benefits:
who forgives all your iniquities,
who heals all your diseases,
who redeems your life from destruction,
who crowns you with lovingkindness
and tender mercies.

PSALM 103:2-4

4. Prayer for Personal Guidance and Discernment

LORD, You have said in Your Word to seek You first every day (Matthew 6:33). "If any of you lacks wisdom, let him ask of God, who gives to all liberally and without reproach, and it will be given to him. But let him ask in faith, with no doubting, for he who doubts is like a wave of the sea driven and tossed by the wind" (James 1:5-6). Lord, I ask You for wisdom and thank You that You will give it to me in abundance. I refuse to doubt Your Word and Your promises to me, so I ask in faith without any doubting. Help me to stand firm on the solid ground of Your Word.

What I specifically need wisdom for today is (name what your greatest need for guidance and discernment is now). The confidence I have in You is that if I ask anything according to Your will, You hear me (1 John 5:14). I bring to You all of my concerns, problems, dreams, needs, fears, longings, and aspirations and ask You to help me pray according to Your will. Show me specifically how to pray about this and show me what to do. Jesus, You said, "If you abide in Me, and My words abide in you, you will ask what you desire, and it shall be done for you" (John 15:7). Help me to live in You and Your Word. Thank You that You hear me and will answer. I cast all my cares on You and leave them in Your hands, knowing they are a weight You do not want me to carry.

I pray for (name of person who needs wisdom and discernment). Help him (her) to make wise decisions and to have the discernment he (she) needs to live safely in this world. Help him (her) to not be wise in his (her) own eyes, but instead to "fear the LORD and depart from evil" as You have instructed in Your Word (Proverbs 3:7). Thank You that "everyone who asks receives, and he who seeks finds, and to him who knocks it will be opened" (Luke 11:10). Give him (her) wisdom regarding what he (she) pursues and help him (her) to seek Your will regarding it. Open the door to what is Your will and close the door to what is not.

You have said, "Delight yourself also in the LORD, and He shall give you the desires of your heart" (Psalm 37:4). My greatest delight is knowing You. I *ask* for Your guidance, *seek* to know your will, and *knock* on the door of Your mercy, confessing that I cannot live without You (Luke 11:9). Thank You that You reward those who seek You first and release their burdens into Your hands. I align myself with You, Lord, and ask You to help me pray as Your Spirit leads me—for myself and for others. Thank You that You hear my prayer and will answer.

In Jesus' name I pray.

I...do not cease to give thanks for you,
making mention of you in my prayers:
that the God of our Lord Jesus Christ,
the Father of glory,
may give to you the spirit of wisdom
and revelation in the knowledge of Him,
the eyes of your understanding being enlightened.

EPHESIANS 1:16-18

5. Prayer for Provision

LORD, I know the enemy can use our finances as a point of attack, so I want to cover them in prayer. I submit myself and my finances and all I have to You. Thank You for the many blessings You have given me. Help me to glorify You in all I do with everything I have. I know all good things come from You. Help me to please You in my paying, giving, buying, and spending.

Your Word says that "the blessing of the LORD makes one rich, and He adds no sorrow with it" (Proverbs 10:22). I pray that the enemy cannot rob and steal from me or my family. Help us to be good stewards of all You have given us. Where I have not been wise, give me guidance. Teach me to give the way You want me to so that in doing so I rebuke the devourer who comes to steal what I have. I resist the enemy who wants to rob us of what You have for us. Help me to make wise financial decisions based on the leading of Your Spirit.

I pray for (<u>name of person who needs provision</u>). Provide for all that she (he) needs. Help her (him) to learn to seek You for everything. Your Word says that "where your treasure is, there your heart will be also" (Matthew 6:21). I pray that her (his) heart would be right before You with regard to finances. Thank You that You will supply everything she (he) needs according to Your riches (Philippians 4:19). Teach her (him) to be grateful for all You provide. Jesus, You have said, "Give, and it will be given to you: good measure, pressed down, shaken together, and running over will be put into your bosom. For with the same measure that you use, it will be measured back to you" (Luke 6:38). Help her (him) to be a generous person and give to You and others in a way that pleases You. Help me to do the same.

Help us to trust in You and not in money or riches. Help us to always be "ready to give, willing to share" (1 Timothy 6:18). Help us to store up "a good foundation for the time to come" (1 Timothy 6:19). Teach us to be wise with everything You give us. Thank You that You always provide for us when we look to You and live Your way.

In Jesus' name I pray.

His delight is in the law of the LORD,
and in His law he meditates day and night.
He shall be like a tree planted by the rivers of water,
that brings forth its fruit in its season,
whose leaf also shall not wither;
and whatever he does shall prosper.

PSALM 1:2-3

6. Prayer for Victory over Enemy Attack

LORD, I thank You that "by You I can run against a troop, by my God I can leap over a wall" (Psalm 18:29). I know that "the wicked plots against the just," but "the Lord laughs at him, for He sees that his day is coming" (Psalm 37:12-13). Thank You that "the adversaries of the LORD shall be broken in pieces; from heaven He will thunder against them" (1 Samuel 2:10). "Now my head shall be lifted up above my enemies all around me" and "I will sing praises to the LORD" (Psalm 27:6).

I praise You in the midst of all trials and challenges, knowing You will do something great in me and in the situation. "The enemy said, 'I will pursue, I will overtake...I will draw my sword, my hand shall destroy them'" (Exodus 15:9). But I say, "Do not rejoice over me, my enemy; when I fall, I will arise; when I sit in darkness, the LORD will be a light to me" (Micah 7:8). "Keep me from the snares they have laid for me, and from the traps of the workers of iniquity. Let the wicked fall into their own nets, while I escape safely" (Psalm 141:9-10). "Let my heart be blameless regarding Your statutes, that I may not be ashamed" (Psalm 119:80).

Reveal to me any place where the enemy is moving in on me, or my family, or anyone else I should pray for who is being attacked by him. I pray for (<u>name of persons you are aware of who are having problems</u>). Show us any situation in our lives where the enemy is trying to work his evil without our even realizing it. Where there is incident after incident of sickness, accidents, or crisis, show us where the enemy is trying to wear us down. I pray that the enemy will not have the satisfaction of manipulating any territory in our lives.

Lord, if any of us are *allowing* the enemy into our lives, reveal it to us. Show us anything that is not right in us that would give the enemy grounds for attack. I know that a person whose walk is blameless will be kept safe, but he whose ways are perverse will suddenly fall (Proverb 28:18). Reveal any way we have allowed thoughts or deeds that are not Your will for us. We want to repent of that and put a stop to all enemy intrusion into our lives.

Lord, we will be victorious because it is You "who shall tread down our enemies" (Psalm 60:12). "You have a mighty arm; strong is Your hand, and high is Your right hand" (Psalm 89:13). "Your right hand, O LORD, has become glorious in power; Your right hand, O LORD, has dashed the enemy in pieces" (Exodus 15:6). Thank You that because of Your mercy You will give us victory over the enemy in every attack he attempts upon our lives.

In Jesus' name I pray.

Do not stay there yourselves,
but pursue your enemies,
and attack their rear guard.
Do not allow them to enter their cities,
for the LORD your God has delivered
them into your hand.

JOSHUA 10:19

7. Prayer for the Hearts of Children

LORD, I pray for every child in my family and the children I know around me to be protected. Specifically, I lift up to You (<u>names of children who are on your heart</u>). Keep the enemy from gaining any ground in their lives in any way. Draw them to You so they will receive You as their Savior before the enemy can erect any stronghold in their lives. For those who have already received You, let the magnitude of what they have done become real to them. Draw them into Your kingdom so they can reject every aspect of evil and darkness, especially as they grow older.

Silence the voice of the enemy to these children so they can hear Your voice. Keep them from all confusion and every plan of the enemy for their lives. Enable them to think clearly and make right choices. Where the enemy has already gained some ground in their lives, I pray You would sever that hold and expose the enemy's lies and tactics. Give me wisdom as to how to pray for the children You have put on my heart.

Lord, I claim the hearts of (<u>names of other specific children who need prayer</u>) for Your kingdom. Turn their hearts toward You. I ask that not one be lost in any way. Keep them protected from the evil one. Hide them from wicked men who would attempt to lead them away from everything You have for them and destroy their lives. I pray Your character will be formed in each child. You have said in Your Word that the children of the righteous will be delivered from the evil one (Proverbs 11:21). I pray these children will be taught by You and they will have great peace (Isaiah 54:13).

Give them the ability to distinguish between good and evil. Engrave Your laws on their heart. I pray they will honor their parents so that they can have a long and good life as is promised in Your commandments (Ephesians 6:1-3). Bring godly friends and influences into their life. Give them discernment about people. Bring back any child who has strayed from Your ways. With regard to that, I pray for (<u>name of child or children</u>). Thank You for Your Word to parents whose children have rebelled against them, which is, "Refrain your voice from weeping, and your eyes from tears; for your work shall be rewarded, says the LORD, and they shall come back from the land of the enemy" (Jeremiah 31:16). Thank You that our work of prayer and intercession will be rewarded. Thank You that Your promise to us is "believe on the Lord Jesus Christ, and *you will be saved, you and your household*" (Acts 16:31). I claim these children for Your kingdom, Lord, and no plan of the enemy can cancel that.

In Jesus' name I pray.

> *There is hope in your future, says the LORD,*
> *that your children shall come*
> *back to their own border.*
>
> JEREMIAH 31:17

8. Prayer for a Safe Place and an End to Violence

LORD, I pray for a place of safety in which to live. Where the place I am living is not safe, I pray You would make it become that way or open up another place that is. If the place I live in is safe, I pray You would always keep it that way. Keep my home safe. Surround it with angels and ward off all evil.

I pray for an end to all crime in my neighborhood, community, and town. Specifically, I pray for the safety of (name persons who are or could be in danger). Keep the enemy far from the area. Where other people have invited him in with their poor choices, pride, arrogance, evil desires, intentions, and practices, I pray You would convict their hearts. If they refuse to acknowledge You in any way, I pray You would cause them to be caught in their own traps. Expose people intent on doing evil *before* they have a chance to commit their crimes. I pray criminals will be put away where they can no longer do harm to others.

Bring an end to violence in (name of place or area where violence or crime is prevalent). I cry out to You on behalf of the people, "for the land is filled with crimes of blood, and the city is full of violence" (Ezekiel 7:23). I pray Your righteousness and goodness would reign over them. Expose the planners of violence before they can commit their evil. I pray violence will no longer be heard in the land. Whoever has evil intent or has demonstrated evil actions against the people there, I pray You would convict their hearts. If their hearts are so hardened against You that they will not hear the truth, if their "pride serves as their necklace" and "violence covers them like a garment" (Psalm 73:6), if they "do not sleep unless they have done evil; and their sleep is taken away unless they make someone fall" and if they "eat the bread of wickedness, and drink the wine of violence"

(Proverbs 4:16-17), I pray their own evil will be turned back on them. You have said that "the violence of the wicked will destroy them, because they refuse to do justice" (Proverbs 21:7). Bring down the instigators of violence against Your people.

Thank You, Lord, that You deliver "me from my enemies. You also lift me up above those who rise against me; You have delivered me from the violent man" (Psalm 18:48). "O GOD the Lord, the strength of my salvation, You have covered my head in the day of battle" (Psalm 140:7). You are "the God of my strength, in whom I will trust; my shield and the horn of my salvation, my stronghold and my refuge; my Savior, you save me from violence" (2 Samuel 22:3). Thank You that "I will lie down in peace, and sleep; for You alone, O LORD, make me dwell in safety" (Psalm 4:8).

In Jesus' name I pray.

When the whirlwind passes by,
the wicked is no more,
but the righteous has an everlasting foundation.

PROVERBS 10:25

9. Prayer for an End to Confusion

LORD, You are "not the author of confusion but of peace" (1 Corinthians 14:33). Where confusion reigns I know the enemy is at work and in charge. I pray there will be no confusion in myself, my family, my relationships, my church, or my work. I pray for clarity and resist the enemy who would come in with confusion. I pray Your peace will reign in these areas instead. I submit to You, Lord, for Your Word says that You have given us a sound mind (2 Timothy 1:7). Thank You for the sound mind of clarity you have promised to those who love You.

I pray You will take away all confusion not only in my mind, but also in the minds of my family, friends, and people I am aware of who are victims of the enemy's tactics of confusion. I pray for an end to all confusion for (name of person or people where confusion reigns). Help her (him, them) to bring every thought captive and under Your control (2 Corinthians 10:5). Help her (him, them) to resist the enemy by refusing to entertain thoughts that are not of You. I pray every place the enemy has brought confusion would be revealed to all concerned. Let the blame be put on the enemy where it belongs. Thank You that You are not the author of confusion, but the enemy is. I resist all confusion from the enemy on behalf of these people. Give them Your sound mind of clarity.

Your Word says that "the tongue is a fire, a world of iniquity. The tongue is so set among our members that it defiles the whole body, and sets on fire the course of nature; and it is set on fire by hell" (James 3:6). Where gossip has brought confusion, expose the works of darkness by the brightness of Your light and evaporate them. I lift up to You (name any specific situation where confusion has entered in through words that have been wrongly spoken). Bring Your truth to bear upon it. For the people who are trying to cause confusion, I pray You will make *them* "drink the wine of confusion" themselves (Psalm 60:3). Give those involved total clarity of thought and the proper perspective. Open blind eyes. Bring revelation where there is confusion and understanding where there is none.

Where the enemy has brought confusion in other parts of the world or in certain people groups, I pray You would bring the clarity of Your truth to bear upon them. Specifically, I pray for (<u>name of people groups, governments, or organizations where confusion reigns</u>). Overturn the workers of confusion and their wrong thinking. Silence those whose lies have caused people to be unable to distinguish between the truth and a lie. May Your truth—the truth of Your Word—break through and reign in the hearts of the people there.

In Jesus' name I pray.

Let them be ashamed
and confounded who seek my life;
let them be turned back and
confused who desire my hurt.

PSALM 70:2

10. Prayer for Freedom from Enemy Harassment

LORD, make me aware of anyone who is being attacked by the enemy and help me to intercede for them the way that You, Jesus, intercede for us. I pray for (<u>name of person who is being harassed by the enemy</u>) and ask that You would bless him (her, me) today. Fill him (her, me) with the knowledge of Your will. Give him (her, me) "wisdom and spiritual understanding" that he (she, I) may walk worthy of You, fully pleasing You, "being fruitful in every good work and increasing in the knowledge" of You (Colossians 1:9-10). Strengthen her (him, me) by Your power. Give him (her, me) all patience and joy (Colossians 1:11). Help him (her, me) to walk worthy of being Your child. I pray he (she, I) will be committed to You and to doing Your will. Give him (her, me) the desire to please You, to be thankful, and to grow in the knowledge of You every day.

Where he (she, I) is being harassed or led astray by the enemy, I pray You would open his (her, my) eyes to the truth. Reveal Yourself and Your plans for his (her, my) life and reveal the enemy's plans and devices as well. Enable him (her, me) to make choices that are right in Your eyes.

Lord, I pray You will pour out Your Spirit on (<u>name of people or people group who need an outpouring of the Spirit on their lives</u>). Enable them to experience a spiritual awakening and have a greater sense of Your presence in their lives. I pray their eyes would be opened to Your truth and all You want to reveal to them. Set them free from every oppression and whatever is keeping them from moving into all You have for them. Give them strength to resist the enemy at all times. Keep them from being anything less than what You call them to be so they can move into all You have for them.

Lord, deliver us out of the enemy's hands. There is freedom in Your presence, so help us to stay close to You. Thank You, Jesus, that

You gave Yourself for us so You "might deliver us from this present evil age, according to the will of our God and Father" (Galatians 1:4). Lord, You said, "Call upon Me in the day of trouble; I will deliver You, and you will glorify Me" (Psalm 50:15). "Deliver us from every evil work" this day (2 Timothy 4:18).

In Jesus' name I pray.

The weapons of our warfare are not carnal but mighty in God for pulling down strongholds, casting down arguments and every high thing that exalts itself against the knowledge of God, bringing every thought into captivity to the obedience of Christ.

2 CORINTHIANS 10:4-5

11. Prayer for Your Leaders

LORD, I pray first of all that You would protect the Christian pastors and leaders in my church and in all Bible-believing churches. Specifically, I pray for (name of Christian leaders who come to mind). Enable them to be a force for good in their community. Help them to always hear clearly from You. Keep them protected from the plans of the enemy, for I know they and their families are targeted by him for destruction.

Bless my church and other churches I know of, such as (name your church and specific churches on your heart right now). Keep them from having a form of godliness but denying its power (2 Timothy 3:5). Keep each church from being people who fail to invite Your Holy Spirit to work in and through them. Help them to live Your way and not their own. Help them to be people who are "praying always with all prayer and supplication in the Spirit, being watchful to this end with all perseverance and supplication for all the saints" (Ephesians 6:18).

I pray if there is error in the leadership of any church that You would expose it so the leader can be corrected. May he or she receive Your correction with repentance and a heart dedicated to serving You.

Keep us all in unity and in peace, serving You only and not ourselves. Teach us how to grow together as a spiritual family and not exclude anyone. You have said much in Your Word about Your people staying together in unity, so I know I must pray for that now. Keep us, the body of Christ, from strife and division that is satanic at its origin. Help us to stand strong in the unity You have called us to.

Lord, I pray for all of the leaders in my community, state, and country to be honest servants of the people. I pray that all corruption would be exposed and the corrupt leaders would be replaced by honest and bright men and women who will do good for the people. Expose every corrupt leader and take him or her out of power. Deliver us from evil in our government.

Enable us to live quiet and peaceful lives free from violence and infighting. Take out leaders who do not care about the people but only their own personal wealth and gain. The issue in my government that is of greatest concern to me is (name issue that concerns you most). I pray that *Your* laws would prevail and the right thing be done. What I want to see done is (tell how you would like to see this resolved). Most of all, I want Your will to be done. Show me how to pray about specific issues so that the infiltration of evil from the enemy will be cast out. Wake up Your believers to serve You with their intercession. Help us to hear Your call and become watchmen on the walls of our community and nation.

In Jesus' name I pray.

I exhort first of all that supplications,
prayers, intercessions,
and giving of thanks be made for all men,
for kings and all who are in authority,
that we may lead a quiet and peaceable life
in all godliness and reverence.
For this is good and acceptable
in the sight of God our Savior.

1 TIMOTHY 2:1-3

12. Prayer for Others to Be Saved

LORD, I pray for the salvation of (name the people you want to receive the Lord). Open the eyes of each one to see Your truth. Reveal Yourself to them and open their heart to receive You, Jesus, as their Savior. Keep me from becoming discouraged if it takes a long time to see a response from someone, for I know Your own brother James apparently did not believe You were who You said You were. It wasn't until after You died and rose from the dead that he was converted. But I know You can draw people to Yourself, and You do it in response to prayer.

You have said, "And I, if I am lifted up from the earth, will draw all peoples to Myself" (John 12:32). I know You don't want anyone to be separated from You and suffering for eternity. You are "long-suffering toward us, not willing that any should perish but that all should come to repentance" (2 Peter 3:9). Because Your desire is for everyone to be saved and "come to the knowledge of the truth" (1 Timothy 2:4), I will continue to pray for the unsaved that they will receive You as their Messiah.

I know "there is no other name under heaven given among men by which we must be saved" (Acts 4:12). "There is one God and one Mediator between God and men," and that is You, "the Man Christ Jesus" (1 Timothy 2:5). I know that "whoever calls on the name of the LORD shall be saved" (Acts 2:21). Thank You that because of Your great love for us that even when we were dead in sin, You made us alive in Jesus by Your grace (Ephesians 2:4-5). For we "all have sinned and fall short" of Your glory (Romans 3:23).

Lord Jesus, You have said, "I am the door. If anyone enters by Me, he will be saved, and will go in and out and find pasture" (John 10:9). "I give them eternal life, and they shall never perish; neither shall anyone snatch them out of My hand" (John 10:28). I pray that the people I have named before You will walk through that door into eternal life and will not be snatched out of Your hand. Help them to hear Your Word and believe it. I pray that even now they cannot be blinded and taken from You by the enemy. I claim them for Your kingdom. Help them to know Your greatest gift to us, which is eternal life with You.

In Jesus' name I pray.

*God so loved the world
that He gave His only begotten Son,
that whoever believes in Him
should not perish but have everlasting life.*

JOHN 3:16

13. Prayer for Racial Unity

LORD, deliver us all from attitudes that are only skin deep. I know the same blood types are found in all races because we all have one and the same heavenly Father. Your Word says, "Have we not all one Father? Has not one God created us? Why do we deal treacherously with one another?" (Malachi 2:10). I wonder that myself, Lord. I pray people will not look down on others for any reason—especially race, skin color, language, appearance, or cultural differences. We resist the evil that is from the enemy of our souls who continue to perpetuate hatred of this sort. Deliver us from this evil and from those who love to stir it up and keep it going.

You have made only two types of people of which we need to make a distinction; and that is *those who know Jesus and are saved,* and *those who do not know Jesus and are not saved.* Enable people to make that clear distinction. Help people to see the beauty You have placed in all races and appreciate the differences. I know that when You call for unity, You make no distinction whatsoever between people except that they be believers. Help us to do the same.

Lord, I pray for peace and unity between believers of all races. If anything but the unconditional love of Christ is shown toward people of any race by anyone, I pray You will convict the hearts of the people who are so blinded. If there is anger or hatred projected toward people of one race toward another race, I pray You would bring the people who perpetrate that evil to their knees before You in repentance. Help us, Your children, to be a people in whom Your love for others reigns. Specifically, I pray about (<u>name persons or people group or situation where discrimination is evident</u>).

Thank You that You are the Father of us all, and in each of us who have received Your Son as Savior Your Holy Spirit dwells. "How good and how pleasant it is" for us to "dwell together in unity!"

(Psalm 133:1). Help us to always "keep the unity of the Spirit in the bond of peace" (Ephesians 4:3). You have made us from one blood, and all of us are redeemed by Your blood. Help us all to love one another the way You have loved us. Help us to sacrifice for one another the way You have sacrificed Yourself for us.

In Jesus' name I pray.

*He has made from one blood every nation of men
to dwell on all the face of the earth,
and has determined their preappointed times
and the boundaries of their dwellings.*

ACTS 17:26

14. Prayer for Exaltation of God

LORD, I worship You as the almighty, all-powerful God of the universe for whom nothing is impossible. There is no one greater than You. No one higher than You. No one more wonderful than You. I exalt You far above all else and give You honor and glory and praise. Thank You that when people deem You worthy of all praise, You save them from their enemies (2 Samuel 22:4). When people praise You, their enemy is defeated (2 Chronicles 20:22).

Thank You that You rescue "the life of the needy from the hands of the wicked" (Jeremiah 20:13 NIV). You give "wisdom to the wise and knowledge to the discerning" and You reveal "deep and hidden things" (Daniel 2:21-22 NIV). You know "what lies in darkness" because You dwell in light (Daniel 2:22). To You belongs all greatness, power, majesty, and splendor (1 Chronicles 29:10-11 NIV). "Let us continually offer the sacrifice of praise to God, that is, the fruit of our lips, giving thanks to His name" (Hebrews 13:15).

Thank You that You inhabit our praise. That's why the enemy hates it. I put on praise to You just like putting on a garment, because when I do, all that the enemy tries to put on me—sorrow, discouragement, anxiety, sadness, and despair—is driven out along with the enemy's plans to destroy me. Thank You, Lord, that with You all things are possible (Matthew 19:26), and You are far greater than any threat of the enemy against me. Help me to remember to make worship of You the first place I turn to when I am confronted by the enemy in my life. Help me to drown out the lies of the enemy by my heartfelt praise.

I give You the glory due Your name, and I worship You in the beauty of Your holiness (Psalm 29:2). I exalt Your holy name and give praise, honor, and worship to You every time I think of You. I love You, Lord, with all my heart, soul, mind, and strength (Mark

12:30). Only You are worthy of glory, majesty, dominion, and power, both now and forever (Jude 1:25). "The Lord is great and greatly to be praised; He is also to be feared above all gods" (1 Chronicles 16:25). I will "sing psalms to Him" and I will "talk of all His wondrous works!" (1 Chronicles 16:9).

In Jesus' name I pray.

I will call upon the Lord,
who is worthy to be praised;
so shall I be saved from my enemies.

2 Samuel 22:4

15. Prayer for Those Who Suffer Persecution

LORD, Your Word says that "all who desire to live godly lives in Christ Jesus will suffer persecution" (2 Timothy 3:12). That is becoming more obvious and blatant every day all over the world, even in my own country. It also says that "evil men and impostors will grow worse and worse, deceiving and being deceived" (2 Timothy 3:13). Give Your believers eyes to see the truth and identify the imposters. Keep us undeceived. Help us to quickly recognize the lies of the enemy and reject them immediately.

I know that one of the most important aspects of spiritual warfare is praying that the gospel message will be spread. Help Your prayer warriors to lay the foundation for that in prayer. I pray as Paul did that I could bring people to Jesus. He was persecuted and even locked up and in chains, yet he prayed to be able to do more to bring people into the kingdom (Colossians 4:3). Help me to be as dedicated to that as he was.

Wherever people are being persecuted by those who do the work of the enemy against those who follow You, I pray You would reach down and rescue them. Specifically, I pray for (<u>name of people or people group who are being persecuted who God brings to mind right now</u>). If they are being threatened, beaten, and abused, I pray You would save them from their captors. Turn the torture on the torturers. I know that though these people are persecuted, You have not forsaken them. Free them from prison, hide them in Your shadow, help them to escape, enable them to find a place of safety, and allow them to bring others to You. Save not only their lives, but also the lives of their family members who are being persecuted as well because they believe in You.

Whoever is in danger right now in any part of the world, I pray You would hear my prayers and set them free from their abusers.

Even if I do not have a specific name, I know You know exactly who and where this prayer should be directed. Specifically, I pray for (name any place where persecution of Christians is happening). Rescue every one of Your people in that area from danger. Protect them from the harm that the enemy intends to inflict on them. Enable them to escape their captors. Where persecution is happening in my own country, I pray you would expose this evil and it would be stopped.

In Jesus' name I pray.

> *We are hard-pressed on every side, yet not crushed;*
> *we are perplexed, but not in despair;*
> *persecuted, but not forsaken;*
> *struck down, but not destroyed.*
>
> 2 CORINTHIANS 4:8-9

16. Prayer for a Clean Heart and Humble Spirit

LORD, I know that "if I regard iniquity in my heart," You will not hear my prayers (Psalm 66:18). I don't want to harbor anything in my heart that hinders my prayers from being answered. Jesus, You have said that, "if we say that we have no sin, we deceive ourselves, and the truth is not in us" (1 John 1:8). *But if we confess our sins, You are "faithful and just to forgive us our sins* and to cleanse us from all unrighteousness" (1 John 1:9). Lord, I ask that You would "search me, O God, and know my heart; try me, and know my anxieties; and *see if there is any wicked way in me*, and lead me in the way everlasting" (Psalm 139:23-24). Show me if there is anything I have said or done that needs to be confessed and repented of before You. I want to be able to say as You do, Jesus, that Satan has nothing in me (John 14:30). This is true of You because *You* were sinless. It is true of *me* because You paid the price for me to be forgiven.

Help me to not sin with my words. I know that "out of the abundance of the heart the mouth speaks" (Matthew 12:34). You have said that "a good man out of the good treasure of his heart brings forth good things, and an evil man out of the evil treasure brings forth evil things" (Matthew 12:35). I know I will have to give account of every word I speak, so I want to confess any careless word I have said (Matthew 12:36). Reveal that to me. Give me a clean and humble heart.

I pray for a clean heart and a humble spirit in (name of person you know who needs to be right with God). I pray that in all his (her) ways he (she) will acknowledge You so You can direct his (her) paths (Proverbs 3:6). I know this is an important part of the process of preparing him (her) for the work You have ahead for him (her) to do.

Lord, I know You have given him (her) a purpose, a calling, and a plan for his (her) life. But he (she) cannot fulfill Your plan without being totally submitted to You in every area of his (her) life. I know that too much of the world in his (her) mind and soul will dilute all understanding of Your purpose for his (her) life. Give him (her) a sense of Your purpose and calling so that he (she) does not get off the path You have for him (her). Keep him (her) from pride and a hard heart so he (she) does not lose the vision You want to give him (her) for the future. Give him (her) a pure heart and a humble spirit so he (she) will not waste time going after something that You will not bless. Help him (her) to "rejoice always, pray without ceasing, in everything give thanks" for then he (she) will be doing Your will (1 Thessalonians 5:16-18).

In Jesus' name I pray.

Create in me a clean heart, O God,
and renew a steadfast spirit within me.
Do not cast me away from Your presence,
and do not take Your Holy Spirit from me.

PSALM 51:10-11

17. Prayer for Strength in the Battle

LORD, I thank You that "You have armed me with strength for the battle; You have subdued under me those who rose against me. You have also given me the necks of my enemies, so that I destroyed those who hated me. They looked, but there was none to save; even to the Lord, but He did not answer them" (2 Samuel 22:40-42). Lord, may Your strength be made perfect in my weakness (2 Corinthians 12:9). I pray that Your power will rest on me, for You are my strength. You are the "strength of my life; of whom shall I be afraid?" (Psalm 27:1). I pray You will pull me out of any net the enemy has laid for me because I rely on Your strength (Psalm 31:4). The specific battle I am facing now is (name the battle you are facing). Help me to stand strong with Your armor on and the weapons You have given me in full use.

Lord, I pray for (name of person who is in a battle with the enemy). Strengthen her (him) with Your strength. Gird her (him) with Your hand of protection. Thank You that You save the righteous because You are our "strength in the time of trouble" (Psalm 37:39). Lord, You have established mountains by Your strength and You have divided the sea by Your strength, so I pray You will establish her (him) with Your strength so that she (he) is immovable (Psalm 65:6, 78:13). You have said, "blessed is the man whose strength is in You," for that person will go from strength to strength (Psalm 84:5,7). I pray You will help her (him) to look to You for Your strength in order to resist the enemy so she (he) can stand strong to the finish.

"My soul, wait silently for God alone, for my expectation is from Him" (Psalm 62:5). Lord, I wait for You, for You are my rock and my defense and I shall not be moved (Psalm 62:6). You are my "refuge and strength, a very present help in trouble" (Psalm 46:1). This is the day that You have made, and I "will rejoice and be glad in it" (Psalm 118:24).

In Jesus' name I pray.

> *Blessed be the* LORD *my Rock,*
> *who trains my hands for war,*
> *and my fingers for battle—*
> *my lovingkindness and my fortress,*
> *my high tower and my deliverer,*
> *my shield and the One in whom I take refuge,*
> *who subdues my people under me.*
>
> PSALM 144:1-2

18. Prayer for Peace in Relationships

LORD, I lift up to You my important relationships. I ask You to bless them with Your peace and love. Where any relationship I have does not glorify You, I pray You will show me clearly. I pray for relationship with my family members and friends. Specifically, I pray for my relationship with (name a family member or friend you are most concerned about). Help us to not seek our own, but "each one the other's well-being" (1 Corinthians 10:24). Help us to "be kindly affectionate to one another with brotherly love, in honor giving preference to one another" (Romans 12:10). Help me to be always forgiving and able to show Your love to another. I pray the enemy cannot put a wedge between us because of our own selfishness.

I pray for the marriages I know of that the enemy is trying to destroy. Specifically, I pray for (name of married couple). Help them (us) to understand how to truly put the other's needs first. I pray for all selfishness and evil attitudes of pride and lack of love to be broken between them (us). Help them (us) to treat one another with love and respect. Enable them (us) to recognize when the enemy has driven a wedge between them (us). Enable them (us) to thwart the enemy's plan to destroy them (us) by living out Your Word in their (our) lives. Enable them (us) to stand strong in resisting the enemy by totally submitting to You. Help them (us) to build one another up and not tear each other down.

Change each one of them (us) to become more like You, and don't let them (us) selfishly cling to what they (we) want when they (we) want it. Teach them (us) to put on the armor of God every day without fail and pray for one another instead of being critical of one another. Help them (us) to plant seeds of love and respect in the marriage so that they will grow into something great. Help them (us) to pull up the seeds of unforgiveness, bitterness, anger, infidelity, and separateness. I pray there will be no divorce in their (our) future. Help them (us) to be united in mutual faith and trust.

Protect their (our) marriage from any lies of the enemy. Help them (us) to take time for one another and to pray together so that the enemy gains no ground between them (us). Help them (us) to "be of the same mind toward one another" (Romans 12:16).

In Jesus' name I pray.

Let all bitterness, wrath, anger,
clamor, and evil speaking
be put away from you, with all malice.
And be kind to one another, tenderhearted,
forgiving one another,
even as God in Christ forgave you.

EPHESIANS 4:31-32

19. Prayer for Deliverance and Freedom

LORD, I know the enemy wants us all to live in condemnation, but You set us free from our sins and the consequences of them if we confess them before You. Specifically, I confess (<u>name any sin you want to confess before God</u>). Thank You that if I confess my sins, You are faithful and just to forgive my sin and to cleanse me from all unrighteousness (1 John 1:9). "O God, You know my foolishness; and my sins are not hidden from You" (Psalm 69:5). Free me from my sins, for they are a heavy burden that is "too heavy for me" (Psalm 38:4). I refuse to allow the enemy of my soul to throw guilt in my face. Your blood on the cross, Jesus, has paid the price for my sins.

Lord, I know that any kind of sin in my life will weaken my prayers. That's why I ask You to reveal anything I need to repent of so I can be free. I know the enemy of my soul will always use my sins against me because unconfessed sin will interfere with my intimacy with You. And that will weaken me in every way. Show me any place in my life where I did not think, speak, or act according to Your standard for my life. (<u>Confess anything the Lord shows you or that you know you have done.</u>) "LORD, be merciful to me; heal my soul, for I have sinned against You" (Psalm 41:4). Forgive me and set me free from them. "I acknowledged my sin to You, and my iniquity I have not hidden. I said, 'I will confess my transgressions to the Lord,' and You forgave the iniquity of my sin" (Psalm 32:5).

Lord, I know we "have been called to liberty" (Galatians 5:13). Help us to "stand fast therefore in the liberty by which Christ has made us free" and not "be entangled again with a yoke of bondage" (Galatians 5:1). I pray specifically for (<u>name of person who needs to be delivered or freed</u>). Set him (her) free from (<u>name what this person needs to be set free of right now</u>). Deliver him (her) of this. Thank You that Your deliverance is always complete. Thank

You that because he (she) is "a new creation; old things have passed away; behold, all things have become new" (2 Corinthians 5:17). Help him (her) to live in that liberty and not be deceived by the enemy again.

In Jesus' name I pray.

If the Son makes you free,
you shall be free indeed.

JOHN 8:36

20. Prayer for Serious Situations in the World

LORD, every day something serious or horrific is happening somewhere in the world and far too often in my own country. It is overwhelming to think about as well as pray about. And there are so *many* concerns that I often don't even know where to start. Yet I know as your prayer warrior You want me to pray for people and situations that are on Your heart as well as mine. I ask that You would show me each day what You want me to pray about. As I hear from You, and also hear of things that are happening in the news, I will pray as You lead me.

The thing that most concerns me now in *my community* is (name the situation and what you want God to do regarding it). Lord, I pray for other situations in *my country* that are troubling. The one that concerns me most is (name the situation and what you would like God to do concerning it). Lord, I pray for the things that are happening in *the world* that are upsetting. I pray for (name the situation and what you would like God to do about it). Give me Your peace about these things.

Lord, I pray for Your peace to reign on earth until such time as You have declared that nations will rise against nations. I know the time is getting shorter, so I pray that people will turn to You and be saved all over the world. I pray they will know that You alone are God and there is no other. I pray Your name will "be great among the nations" because You will pour out Your Spirit on everyone (Malachi 1:11). I pray especially for (name the area of the world that most concerns you right now and what you want to see God do there). I pray You would pour out Your Spirit upon the people in that area and reveal Your truth to them. Your Word says that "the LORD brings the counsel of the nations to nothing; He makes the plans of the peoples of no effect" (Psalm 33:10). Bring to nothing all

plans of the enemy to destroy Your people. I pray especially about
people who are haters of Your people. Specifically, I pray You would
destroy the plans of (name the people groups who spout hatred and
support the murder of innocent people). Expose the plots of these
people before they can carry out their evil plans.

I see that nothing that is wrong in this world can be made right
outside of You. No conflict can ever be solved and no place of safety
can ever be established without You. You are the solution to every
problem. Only Your love and peace can ever answer to our desperate need. Come, Lord Jesus, deliver us from evil, make Your face to
shine upon us and give us peace.

In Jesus' name I pray.

I will praise You, O Lord, among the peoples;
I will sing to You among the nations.
For Your mercy reaches unto the heavens,
and Your truth unto the clouds.
Be exalted, O God, above the heavens;
let Your glory be above all the earth.

PSALM 57:9-11